SINGING SOLDIERS

SINGING SOLDIERS

By
JOHN J. NILES

ILLUSTRATED BY
MARGARET THORNILEY WILLIAMSON

CHARLES SCRIBNER'S SONS
NEW YORK · LONDON
1927

TO THE
AMERICAN NEGRO SOLDIERS
WHO MADE
THIS WRITING POSSIBLE

BY WAY OF INTRODUCTION

On my first trip to Paris as a member of the A. E. F. (it was in December, 1917) I ran onto a paper-bound volume of French war-songs by Monsieur Théodore Botrel, titled "Les Chants du Bivouac."

Monsieur Botrel, known to the French as "Chansonnier des Armées," had been commissioned by the Ministry of War, then headed by Millerand, to sing and recite certain songs and poems of a patriotic nature to the French soldiers. His book, "Les Chants du Bivouac," was a collection of these. The work contained more than a hundred pen illustrations by Carlègle and a preface by a member of the Académie Français, Monsieur Maurice Barrès. At my hotel in the Rue Richelieu, just around the corner from the Rue St. Anne M. P. jail, I took "Les Chants du Bivouac" to the piano, and, with the help of a French aviator in our party, sang some of the songs.

That night I decided to borrow M. Botrel's idea and attempt a collection of United States Army war-songs—to make as nearly as possible an unexpurgated record of the words and to write off the tunes whenever I had time and music-score paper. My resolution at first was intended to include any songs sung by the soldiers of the United States Army, but the imagination of the white boys did not, as a rule, express itself in song. They went to Broadway for their music, contenting themselves with the ready-made rhymes and tunes of the professional song-writers—song-writers who for reasons best avoided now did not give up their royalty

checks for the chance to secure the safety of democracy at
thirty-three dollars per month.

After a little while I discovered that time, music-score
paper, and original songs were rare. In fact, I was even be-
ginning to lose interest in my musical diary, when we encountered some negro troops. True, they sang some music-
hall ditties—after all, those colored regiments were recruited
from every corner of the United States—there were Harlem
negroes, Texas negroes, negroes from south-side Chicago,
negroes from North Carolina—negroes, as they so aptly
said, "frum all over." Usually, among the black troops,
there were a few semi-professional musicians who did the
music-hall stuff as we see it done nowadays in the black-
and-tan cabarets and supper clubs. And then there were
the others, the natural-born singers, usually from rural dis-
tricts, who, prompted by hunger, wounds, homesickness, and
the reaction to so many generations of suppression, sang the
legend of the black man to tunes and harmonies they made
up as they went along—tunes and harmonies ofttimes too
subtle for my clumsy fingers and my improvised score paper.

At last I had discovered something original—a kind of
folk music, brought up to date and adapted to the war situations—at the same time savoring of the haunting melodic
value found in the negro music I had known as a boy in
Kentucky.

In the early summer of 1918 I gave up recording the songs
of white boys and began to put myself out of the way to
find a chance to come in contact with the negro soldier, who,
as far as possible, put a little music into everything he did,
be it marching, digging, cooking, travelling, unloading ships,
or any of the thousand and one jobs soldiers always have
to do. The negro soldier not only had the mellow, resonant

vocal qualities so necessary in singing, but he had abandon and an emotional nature which, with his ability to dramatize trivial situations, many times produced the most affecting performances.

My duty as a pilot in the United States Air Service took me by air and rail to practically every area occupied by American troops, and as I knew I would be encountering negroes wherever our soldiers were established, my musette bag always contained a piece of score-paper or something I might hastily convert by drawing a few staffs and a clef.

Whatever may be said for the negro as a fighting soldier, no one may gainsay him as a singing soldier, nor discount the fact that his music had some part in the success gained by our arms in the past war.

The gathering and compiling of the matter in this volume covered a period of seven years. It is natural to suppose that I received advice and assistance from many sources. Mrs. Harriet Ayer Seymour, Mr. E. von der Goltz, Mr. Marshall Bartholomew, Mr. N. C. Page, Mr. Max Marks, Mr. Douglas Moore, Mr. O. B. Judson, and Mr. W. H. Handy, the "Blues" authority, supplied me with technical, legal, and musical information. Lieutenant Lee Turner, an artilleryman, and Lieutenant J. Heath Brasselman, a machine-gunner, both having made the war with the A. E. F., supplied me with military data, maps, and information, supplementing my own diaries. From Mr. Brian Brown's book, "The Wisdom of the Hindus," I have, with Mr. Brown's permission, reprinted a verse of the "Bhagavad-Gita," as translated from the Sanskrit by Sir Edwin Arnold.

I have unconsciously taken so much from Mr. Pierre A. Bernard (Shastri), Nadia, India, of the Royal Asiatic Society of Great Britain and Ireland, American Philological Society, New York Academy of Science, etc., etc., that to him I am perhaps most indebted—not for music nor forgotten dates and places, but for an unlimited amount of encouragement and a better understanding of the fitness of things.

NYACK, N. Y., *November*, 1926.

LIST OF SONGS

CHAPTER I

THE first entry into my diary of War Music was made in Issoudun (Indre), France, where I had been sent with a detachment of American Aviation Cadets to study the art of flying. That winter of 1917–1918 we did very little work in the air—we dug trenches, latrines, and stood guard duty, for the Issoudun camp was not completed. In fact, it was humorously referred to as the muddiest hole in France, where flying was a promise. A camp newspaper known as the *Plane News* was being published "from time to time"—a newspaper on which I was serving as associate editor. One night in December, 1917, in the *Plane News* office, during one of our "after-taps copy-writing sprees," a cadet came in with a contribution which proved to be the verses of a song about "going home." It wasn't entirely original, but every verse told volumes of truth. In the fall of 1918, at a flying-field near Toul, I encountered some men who sang the same tune with a new set of verses, the earlier ones having disappeared. Their rhymes were about Air Service activities, but I did not consider them interesting enough to record.

Here are seven verses of the song as it was sung in Issoudun during the winter of 1917–1918—the first song I recorded in my "Singing Soldiers" manuscript.

I want to go home—I want to go home—
The treatment is awful—the food is a joke—
If you want to pass out, just come here and you'll croak.
So, send me over the sea—

GOING HOME SONG

This melody is not entirely original—it reminds one faintly of such tunes as "Take me out to the ball game," "The Bowery," "Yip I Yaddie I Yeh," etc.

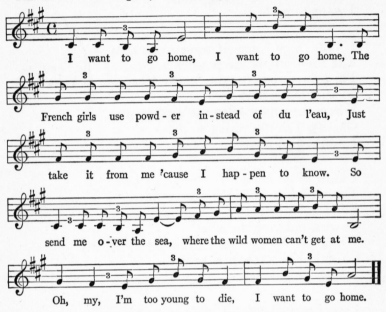

I want to go home, I want to go home, The
French girls use powd-er in-stead of du l'eau, Just
take it from me 'cause I hap-pen to know. So
send me o-ver the sea, where the wild women can't get at me.
Oh, my, I'm too young to die, I want to go home.

Where the Top Sergeants can't get at me—
Oh, my, I'm too young to die—
I want to go home.

I want to go home—I want to go home—
I don't want to go in the trenches no more—
Where hand-grenades and whiz-bangs they roar.
So send me over the sea,
Where the Heinies they can't get at me—
Oh, my, I'm too young to die—
I want to go home.

I want to go home—I want to go home—
It's always a raining—the mud is knee-deep—
The lice are so active, I never can sleep—

So send me over the sea,
Where the Top Sergeants can't get at me—
Oh, my, I'm too young to die—
I want to go home.

I want to go home—I want to go home—
The French girls use powder in place of "de l'eau"—
I'm telling you straight, 'cause I happen to know—
So send me over the sea—
Where the wild women can't get at me,
Oh, my, I'm too young to die—
I want to go home.

I want to go home—I want to go home—
The war ain't so bad if you're wearin' a star—
But bein' a private don't get you so far.
So send me over the sea,
Where the tin hats they can't get at me—
Oh, my, I'm too young to die—
I want to go home.

I want to go home—I want to go home—
In place of a dinner they pass us out slum—
My whole inner workings have gone on the bum—
So send me over the sea,
Where the Mess Sergeants can't get at me—
Oh, my, I'm too young to die—
I want to go home.

I want to go home—I want to go home—
I don't want to fly in a wiggly winged Sop—
They act like a buzzard just ready to drop—
So send me over the sea—
Where the monitors can't get at me—
Oh, my, I'm too young to die—
I want to go home.

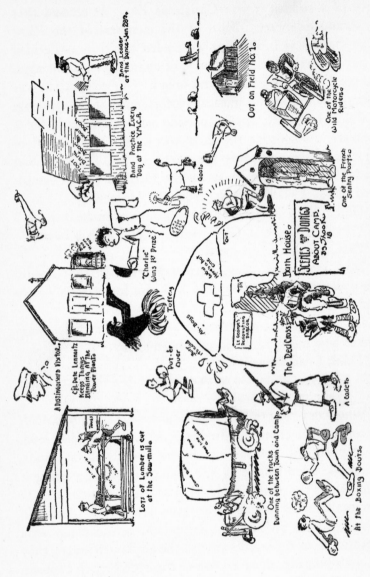

THIS IS A REPRINT FROM THE *PLANE NEWS*, JANUARY, 1918

The artist, Cadet Bill Shook, from Indianapolis, Indiana, made the drawings from life.

4

All of a sudden it was Christmas Eve. It seemed that we should celebrate. Most of the members of the *Plane News* staff were broke, but we pooled our francs—decided to buy a bottle of rum, a bottle of champagne, a few eggs, and steal a supply of milk and bread. Our celebration was planned to follow the musical performance of the evening, in which I had to appear playing accompaniments for a violinist. As soon as the show was over I was elected to buy the liquor and start the party. Oley, "the big bad Swede" (who was on duty at the German prison camp), spied me as I was returning from the canteen.

"Halt! Who goes there? Sing it out and make it quick."

"Why—why—hello, Oley—why—friend with a bottle."

"Pass, friend! Halt, bottle!"

"Now look here, Oley, have a heart with that bottle. You wall-eyed liquor-guzzler, a hell of a lot of good you're doin' in this man's army."

Oley was calculating with the keen eye of a professional drinker how much he could take bottoms up.

"Think I can make it?"

He grasped the bottle with both hands—the uppermost marking the new low level.

"Why, Oley, you rum-befuddled goovus, I'll bet you don't remember your orders." We drank deep. We laughed loud. We slapped one another on the back—and shook hands. This drinking and slapping had been going on all evening— by midnight the guard would be in prime condition.

It was Christmas Eve—Christmas Eve, 1917. Although the guards who walked post around the prison camp were separated from the details around the airplane hangars, they had the advantage of being nearer the little French canteen. Nearly all the liquor-laden boys had to pass the prison camp

—that's how the prison guards did so much free drinking. The German prisoners hauled garbage and dug trenches. Some of them did K. P. in the cadets' mess—calm-looking, blond fellows with little pill-box hats, who lived in a separate camp—guarded by a detail of French and Americans.

It was Christmas Eve in the muddiest hole in France— The moon was full, and, shining through the leafless trees, cast an intricate pattern of black on the white of the snow-covered ground.

Oley was on duty again from ten to twelve. He had just sampled a swig or two of "niggerhead" rum out of a bottle wrapped around with straw. It was my bottle—the first one hadn't been nearly enough.

"Ought to stick around, Jack, old walrus. The Heinies are goin' to sing. They've been practising every night for some time. Ole Caspard says they is a famous piano-player among 'em; he leads 'em, and say, I think you'd like to hear 'em. Don't have no piano—got a little brass pipe—makes a noise like a peanut whistle. He starts 'em off and they do the rest."

It was near midnight when the prisoners actually began to sing. They had been permitted to move some of the tables from one end of their mess hall. Their audience numbered four: Caspard, the Corporal of the French Guard, one French private, Oley, the American Guard, and myself. We had been sitting outside the enclosure near a sentry-box, listening to the D'Artagnan-like reminiscences of Caspard, when through the thin walls of the barracks came the kind of music one hears only in dreams:

Stille Nacht, heilige Nacht,
Alles schlaft, einsam wacht

Nur das traute Hochheilige Paar,
Holder Knabe im lochtigen Haar,
Schlaf in himmlischer Ruh,
Schlaf in himmlischer Ruh.

Had these men been our enemies? Were they really prisoners of war? Were they the sullen, glum-looking fellows who
hauled garbage and cleaned latrines? Had I been trans-
ported by the rum? In my wildest imaginings, I had never
conceived a more gloriously balanced group of male voices.
I had listened to "Die Meistersinger," to "Tristan," to the
King's prayer and the accompanying choruses at the end of
the first act of "Lohengrin." I had sung "The Messiah,"
"Elijah," and "Judas Maccabeas," but this—the singing of
a simple carol—left me inarticulate. The tune was familiar—
I had sung it as a boy:

Silent night, holy night.
All is calm, all is bright. . . .

The others too were moved. I could see Oley's face against
the moonlight. The silly, drunken grin was gone. With his
hands on the butt of his rifle (the bayonet end stuck down
in the ground), he stood very still. The French private had
deserted his sentry box—he had drawn nearer the prisoners'
barracks, so that he might not miss any of the singing. As
the singers paused between two verses, Caspard spoke:

Tiens! quelles voix!
Quelles pensées derrière ces voix!
Ils pensent à leurs foyers—
À leurs foyers la-bas en Allemagne—
Comment moi, je pense à mon chez-moi qui était la-bas à
    Soissons!
La guerre! La guerre!

He dug his heel viciously into the half-frozen mud and, pulling himself to his feet, began to walk up and down. His hands joined behind his back. His head dropped in meditation. And those voices again singing:

Stille Nacht, heilige Nacht.

One verse was sung so softly that we could scarcely hear it through the walls of the barracks. Were these men our enemies? Had the Sarajevo incident really made them so? Did unrestricted submarine warfare get us into this muddle? Perhaps it was the *Lusitania!* I wanted to cry out aloud against something that was all wrong.

Caspard sat down beside me—he was an old man. His home in Soissons had been destroyed. The dash of the D'Artagnan was gone. He wept softly. Great God! what a situation! But what could we do about it? Nothing. We were caught in a grotesque, unromantic, unheroic, mechanical war. The only thing for us to do was to make the most of it—to laugh as long as we could laugh and save our tears for a crisis. All the while the prisoners were singing:

Stille Nacht, heilige Nacht,
Alles schlaft, einsam wacht.

I thought how far the singing of this almost divine carol had transcended the power of their arms.

Nur das traute Hochheilige Paar,
Holder Knabe im lochtigen Haar,
Schlaf in himmlischer Ruh,
Schlaf in himmlischer Ruh.

They later sang some livelier things—one about the wedding of grandmother and grandfather. But the others I have forgotten against the glorious memory of the singing of "Silent Night."

All the talent in camp had been rehearsing for a black-face minstrel show, to be given Christmas night. I had been delegated by Captain Kearney to organize the show and see to the matters of production. We were to have a regular old style oleo with specialties, singing and dancing numbers, original ditties, local jokes, etc. Among the numbers that missed fire was a song proposed to me by a driver in one of the Motor Transport outfits. Charley planned to open his act with a limerick.

> Now Jonah told the wildest tales—
> Of accidents in ships with sails—
> The worn-out wheeze
> Of the moon and the cheese—
> Of mutinies and man-eatin' whales.

Then he intended to "go into his number" (as the vaude-villians say). One of the boys in his outfit, a back-room-of-a-saloon pianist, had worked out a simply harmonized accompaniment. They had borrowed their tunes from reliable sources and manufactured the lyrics out of current lingo of the service. Jonah was a private in the United States Army. The song recounted the unfortunate details of his mortal combat with the whale. The legendary Jonah yarn got into the song only by supplying the names of the dramatis personæ.

Now gather round me, brothers, and to you I'll tell a tale,
About a soldier-boy named Jonah and a great sea-going
    whale—
How the whale he bucked and Jonah ducked—
And the whale said, well I will be shucked—
Oh, that's the story of Jonah and the great sea-going whale.

WHALE SONG

This soldier boy had gone to reliable Irish sources for his melody.

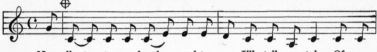

Now lis-ten to me, brothers, and to you I'll tell a tale, Of a

sol - dier boy named Jonah and a great sea - go - in' whale— How the

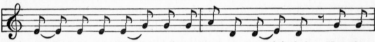

whale he bucked and Jonah ducked and the whale said, "Well I will be shucked," Now

D. C.

that's the sto - ry of Jo - nah and the great sea - go - in' whale.

Now Jonah pulled the bolt back and he shoved home a
    shell,
And said, I'll blow this bloody whale all the way to Hell,
But the whale he bucked and Jonah ducked
And the whale said well I will be shucked—
Oh, that's the story of Jonah and the great sea-going whale.

Then Jonah got himself a piece of field-artillery,
And said he'd shoot a hole into that whale's great big belly—
But the whale he bucked and Jonah ducked
And the whale said well I will be shucked,
Oh, that's the story of Jonah and the great sea-going whale.

Oh, Jonah got a gas-bomb and said this is the nuts,
I'll polish off this monster, cause I surely hate his guts,
But the whale he bucked and Jonah ducked
And the whale said well I will be shucked,
Oh, that's the story of Jonah and the great sea-going whale.

Then Jonah got a minnenwafer right from Germany
And said of that terrific whale I'll surely rid the sea.
But the whale he bucked and Jonah ducked
And the whale said well I will be shucked,
Oh, that's the storv of Jonah and the great sea-going whale.

Now from the cook shack Jonah took a mess pail full of bill,
He thot he'd try to poison what he couldn't kill,
But the whale he bucked and Jonah ducked
And the whale said well I will be shucked,
Oh, that's the story of Jonah and the great sea-going whale.

Then Jonah threw a mills bomb right at the monster's head,
The mills bomb ricocheted and cooled Jonah off instead—
'Cause the whale he bucked and Jonah ducked
And the whale said well I will be shucked,
Oh, that's the story of Jonah and the great sea-going whale.

But Charley lost his nerve at the last moment and in spite of a generous issue of milk-punch (which was 90 per cent punch), he couldn't make up his mind to go on. The minstrel show had to function without the Jonah song. One night in the *Plane News* office, Charley sang fifteen verses of his song to me—some of them were deliciously obscene. The seven verses recorded were for public performance, where a mixed audience might be encountered.

We ran into strange difficulties with our Christmas performance. The use of one of the welfare organizations' buildings was a point in question. The welfare secretary (a male person of past middle-age) told me at first that we positively could not use the building. He didn't mind musical evenings, where authorized welfare workers, etc., performed, but black-face minstrels—no! Sometime before, a similar show had been given and some of the performers had got very drunk—it was too much of a disgrace to be repeated. I passed this yarn on to Captain Kearney and Colonel Kilner—you can imagine what they told me I might do if I found it necessary.

Needless to say, we used the welfare workers' building, and through an over-consumption of the aforementioned milk-punch, several of the performers did their stuff in a marvellously abandoned manner—one of them passing out during the performance—much to the amusement of the audience.

Most of the welfare workers associated with the United States Army—Protestants, Catholics, and Jews—brought their theological ideas of priesthood along with them as part of their baggage. These dispensers of "universal truth" couldn't forget their heaven-sent responsibility of saving the world—not even long enough to let a bunch of homesick soldiers have a fine, large, and very harmless evening. Some school-teaching, mystic practices of theology had armed them with what it took to "save the world"—but few did I meet who were able to solve their own problems or to live their own lives in a manner that brought much acclaim from themselves or from others.

CHAPTER II

THE "Going Home Song" and the song about Jonah and the whale were the only bits of music recorded in 1917.

Early in 1918 I went with a detachment of Americans to Foggia, Italy, where we learned to fly French Farmans and Italian Colombos under the direction of Italian instructors.

TWENTY-EIGHT-METRE NIEUPORT

From Italy we were sent north to the Second Aviation Instruction Centre at Tours, France, where we flew the Caudron tractors with Anzani radial motors in them. Several of our boys were disabled flying the Caudrons, but no one was killed. From Tours we went back to Issoudun. The camp had changed some; there were many new faces—and many new crosses in the graveyard. At Issoudun we flew Nieuports; first the 23-metre ones with 80 horse-powered

motors, then 18-metre ones, and, finally, the 15-metre ones
with 120 horse-power. It was our first experience with rotary
motors. It was also our first experience with ships requiring
delicate control. Many of our good boys came down—we
buried some of the most promising men in the outfit. Mysterious things happened at Issoudun—one captain, who was
a member of the local committee to investigate crashes, was
sent on one hour's notice to a camp in another part of France
because he seemed to be alarmed about the death-rate. A
satisfactory reason was never given for the flourishing condition of the graveyard.

From Issoudun I was sent to Orly (Seine), a flying-field
not far from Paris. It was known in the A. E. F. as AAAP
No. 1 (American Aviation Acceptance Park No. 1). From
Orly we flew to nearly all the flying-fields in France, deliver-
ing all kinds of ships—fighting ships, school ships, observation ships, gunnery-practice ships, etc. In flying to the
aviation base nearest the front, Collombey les Belles, we
made one stop—Vinets—a gas and oil filling-station, where
we could stop over night if we found it too dark or too foggy
to make Collombey les Belles. One night at Collombey les
Belles, while at mess, an officer (detailed to technical re-
search) asked me if I would like to accompany him in a trip
up nearer the front to recover the remains of a German
plane that had just fallen a while before dark. We should
be able to make the trip and get back to the Toul Station in
time to catch the midnight train to Orly.

After two hours and a half of dragging along traffic-
crowded roads, we arrived at the scene of the crash. In
spite of the guard placed on the German ship, many things
valuable from a technical point of view were gone—the
souvenir collectors had done their stuff. The pilot had been

taken in a dying condition to a near-by field hospital. My friend the technical expert decided to see if he could gain any information from him, so we visited the roadside hospital. It was nearly dawn when we started back. During the night a medical corporal, who had a rare sense of narration, related some of his experiences to me. Among them, he told of a negro who had died singing snatches of a song.

The black boy had been brought into the hospital in a semidelirious condition—he believed himself still able to drive his team of mules. He wanted to leave the hospital and return to his ammunition train. He resisted the efforts of the stretcher-bearers and the medics.

"Lay off me, white man—lay off, I tells you, lay off me. I wants to go back—I wants to git out o' here."

"Shut up, shut up" (a voice from the other end of the tent), "you can't go anywhere. Hell, you can't even walk."

"All de same I knows what I wants."

"Say, medic, pipe 'im down. Give 'im a shot in 'is arm."

"Aw, let 'im alone, he ain't botherin' you."

"The hell he ain't."

"I wants to go back, I duz. I wants to git out o' here."
The medical corporal turned to the colored boy.

"So you want to go up where they're fightin', eh? One would think you'd had enough."

"I ain't botherin' so much 'bout de fightin', Mr. Medical Man; what I wants to do is to go where dat dead sergeant is."

An irritable white boy with a bandaged head had listened to as much as he could.

"Well, you'll go and if you're not careful, you'll go in a whale of a hurry. He's been tellin' us he killed 'is sergeant."

"Oh Lordy, oh Lordy" (his voice was not much more than a whisper), "I asks you—I asks you to smite me down if I did it a purpose."

The white boy with the bandaged head was seized with something akin to terror.

"Steady now, black boy, steady, don't go havin' no sleight-o'-hand conversations with God 'bout knockin' you off. He might do a good job and knock me off with you. Every time I stop thinkin' 'bout anything else, I can see a Heinie, writin' so peaceful-like in a little book, just before my grenade hit 'im."

The medical corporal listened as he administered to the colored boy—listened carefully—he'd use this talk in a play some time—the medical corporal administering to the colored boy as gently as he could, considering the number of men to be cared for. In fact, individual care was almost impossible (and the wounded were wise enough to know this), for there were rows and rows of cots and improvised beds on which Frenchmen, Americans, and Germans lay tossing and suffering from wounds that grew more feverish, more unbearable as the night wore slowly on. There were men sitting on the ground or on rough benches, leaning against walls. Their eyes were bandaged—they had been gassed.

They were waiting turns to be evacuated. Those field hospitals and dressing stations—God!

Friend, did you ever smell a field hospital—after it had stood all day under a blistering summer sun—with newly turned mounds all about—where the burial squads had stowed the festering dead of a rapidly retreating enemy— where this year's barrages have burrowed into the tortured countryside and spewed the half-rotten contents of last year's graves—where the sweaty, unwashed smell of sick and wounded men is strangely blended with the odor of disinfectants and chemicals — where the blazing sun has warmed the newly clustered graves until they almost seem to breathe?

A CATCH OF HEINE SOUVENIRS

This outfit was housed in the remains of a roadside hotel, a barn, part of a church, and the near-by parish house. The non-coms had moved their cots to a temporary shelter some distance away for the benefit of quiet. When all the other spaces were occupied by wounded, the non-coms' quarters were taken by the overflow.

At one end of the shelter two grievously wounded Germans carried on delirious conversations with friends back home. The colored boy near by had propped up his head. Between the singing of a line or two of a song he had brought

from the Southland, he would declare again his desire to go
back to the sergeant who was dead. Next lay the white boy
who saw visions of the German writing in the little book.
And beyond him a medical corporal, whose body ached—
whose temples throbbed—whose throat was dry. He could-
n't seem to remember how long it had been since he had

THE COLORED BOY WAS A WAGONER

slept—really slept. He tried to think how wonderful it
would be when the classes assembled at school in the fall.
He listened to the colored boy—he'd remember what that
fellow said and use it in one of the college plays some time.

The colored boy was a wagoner—a driver in a supply
train. They had been passing over shell-swept roads with
unusually good luck—then the Boche treated them to a
bombing raid. The supply train was stopped—all hands lay
flat on the roadside. One of the teams became excited—it

wouldn't do to have a wagon in the ditch. There was a call for help. Under a sergeant's direction, the wagoner lay where he was—the sergeant would see what could be done. He hadn't more than stood up when a bomb struck the road. It was one of those instantaneous types of aerial bombs that burst about two feet off the ground. One lying flat might miss the dispersion of the burst. The sergeant was cut in two. Other bombs fell. The wagoner was wounded, but he blamed himself for the death of the sergeant.

The medical corporal had another hour in which he might rest. He lighted a candle, made sure the shelter flaps were closed, and produced a stub of lead-pencil. The negro boy spoke less of the dead sergeant. He was singing ever so softly:

> Don't close dose gates, 'cause I'm sure comin' in,
> Don't close dose gates, 'cause I'm sure comin' in.

"Say, friend, can't you do something fur 'im? The shine, I mean. He's gone to singin'. An' what de hell does 'unser' mean? One of the Boche's been blabbin' about 'unser' till I'm about to go dippy myself. 'Unser, unser'—Jesus, will he ever die and be quiet!"

The medical corporal was writing:

> Don't close dose gates, 'cause I'm sure comin' in—
> Don't close dose gates, 'cause I'm sure comin' in—
> Peter, take your hand off de handle ob dat gate—
> 'Cause I'm sure comin' in—
> Jesus said he wouldn't mind if I was a little late,
> When he pardoned me my sins.

The tune was simple—he'd write down what he could of it. Why hadn't people invented a shorthand system for music? Musicians were behind time.

Don't close dose gates, 'cause I'm sure comin' in—
Don't close dose gates, 'cause I'm sure comin' in—
Some folks says dat heaven is a white man's place,
But I'm sure comin' in—
Good Book says it doesn't matter 'bout de color ob
     your face,
So I'm sure comin' in.

The tune was simple—he'd take down what he could of it and sing the rest to some one who could help him write it off according to Hoyle. Funny about not having shorthand for music.

"Unser Heiliger Gott—warum—warum habe ich? Warum?"

"Listen, pardner, hey you, medic, won't you, for God's sake, for God's sake, do something fur the poor Heinie bastard? Give 'im a shot in 'is arm, er give me one."

Don't close dose gates, 'cause I'm sure comin' in—
Don't close dose gates, 'cause I'm sure comin' in—

Toward morning the colored boy was quiet—and the German's God seemed to have answered his prayer, too.

Some of the most homesick days I ever experienced were spent at Orly (Seine), and I've never been able to tell why. It was a very romantic piece of French countryside. A few miles away, at Choisy le Roi, during the Reign of Terror, revolutionists had destroyed palaces and chateaux belonging to the Louis,—palaces and chateaux, where kings and courtiers had disported themselves in the most dissolute manner. West of our camp ran the Fontainebleau road, the road that connected the palace in Fontainebleau with the palaces in Paris. A few miles farther west lay Versailles, which from the air looked like a fairy garden—a fairy garden, indeed, with its palaces and its cross-shaped lake.

DON'T CLOSE DOSE GATES

ARRANGED BY J. J. N.

Don't close dose gates, 'cause I'm sure comin' in, Don't close dose gates, 'cause I'm sure comin' in.

Pe - ter, take your hand off de han - dle ob dat gate, 'Cause

I'm sure com - in' in. Je - sus said he would-n't mind if I

D.C.

was a lit - tle late When he par-doned me my sin. Don't

We had some lively dances at Orly every now and then, but even so, it was a lonesome place. Fortunately we were away most of the time—either flying to some distant camp or waiting for flying weather, because bright, clear days were rare in the fall of 1918. During a protracted rainy spell we made friends with the officers of a colored labor battalion, engaged in repairing the Fontainebleau road. Their officers, welcome guests at Sanger Hall, had promised to show off the battalion in a drawing-room set and thereby prove their superiority over the average run of low-type gravel haulers and road menders. The performance would be staged at Sanger Hall.

Sanger Hall was a gift to the officers at the Orly Flying Field. Captain Sanger had lost his life while flying at Orly. His wife, to honor her husband, had equipped a barracks in a most luxuriant manner, named it "Sanger Hall," and opened its doors as a free club-house. It was like stumbling upon a Taj Mahal in the middle of the desert—divans, fire-places, a library, piano, soft carpets, dim lights, little cur-tains puckered up at the windows—what a place was Sanger Hall!

The show opened with a crap game. One of the players was more dishonest than players usually are in army games of chance.

"Stop dices!"

"How you git dis stop?"

"You're holdin'. Pass dose dices up agin yonder blanket. I ain't goin' to see no dice-holdin' high-brown spendin' my dicks franc notes." (Fr. dix.)

"Say, lad, you're talkin' purty hard, ain't you?"

"Hard? Did you say hard?* Why, boy, do you know who I am? Well, I'll tell you. Dey is only two real hard

* Besides being hard, this colored boy had blue lips and boasted of a poisonous bite.

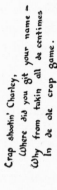

Crap shootin' Charley,
Where did you git your name —
Why from takin all de centimes
In de ole crap game.

men in dis here United States Army of America, and fo'
God, I'se both ob 'em."

The crap game was an overture to a scene involving a
flying officer and a negro soldier. The flying officer (this
part was played by one of the colored boys) had just invited a number of enlisted men to ride with him. One colored boy among those invited refused to ride.

"Nossar, I declines de honor. I don't mean to hab my
friends standin' round, singin', 'Hallelujah, hardly knew
you.' Nossar. I believe you is, sure God, a regular pilot.
But I've seen dose gasoline engines stop before now. It 'ud
jes' be my luck to hab to git out an' crank when we wuz
'bout 2,000 miles up. Nossar, I don't crank no airship while
it's aflyin'. Not me!"

This scene was very much applauded, particularly by the
pilots who were tight. "And now, gentlemen, may we present Mr. Mooney Dukes, assisted by us all, singin' 'Hoochey,
Coochey Hilda' and 'Crap-Shootin' Charley'."

The song about Hilda was reminiscent of a thousand
"blues songs" where a male is pleading for the privilege of
returning to some happy home he had deserted, for reasons
he hoped no one would remember.

> Hoochey, Coochey Hilda, won't you take me back—
> I knows I'se done you wrong—
> I come to France to make de Kaiser ball de Jack—
> Now you jus' got to take me back.
> Hoochey, Coochey Hilda, I knows I'se done you wrong.

This song, in spite of its many amusing verses, failed, because
the boy at the piano banged so that the singing became incidental to the accompaniment. As an encore to the "Hoochey,
Coochey" song, the boys sang five couplets (in a quasi-quartette
form) to the famous old tune of "Ashes to Ashes, Dust to Dust."

Goin' to lay myself down on de railroad track,
An' let de steam cars roll over my big black back.
(Then follows the usual two-line chorus.)

French cannon-ball goes so goddam fast,
Can't never count de cars as they wizzes past,
(Chorus.)

THE SINGING BECAME INCIDENTAL TO THE ACCOMPANIMENT

Goin' to let my insurance policy lapse,
Cause I can't spend no jack after de bugler plays taps,
(Chorus.)

German throwed down his gun and started in cryin',
And took off fer Berlin a Hell firin', yellin', and flyin',
(Chorus.)

Goin' to git myself a French gal wid nice smooth flanks,
An' tell her de blacks is de best o' de Yanks,
(Chorus.)

The crashing hit of the evening came later when they sang the song about "Crap-Shootin' Charley." The "Hilda" song had warmed up Mooney's voice. After a whispered conversation with the boy at the piano, they began:

All I needs is twenty francs,
Come on, bones, and treat me nice.
Papa's lookin' for a natural,
Roll 'em, soldier, roll dose dice.

O, crap-shootin' Charley, where did you git yo' name?
Why, from takin' all de centimes in de ole crap game.
O, crap-shootin' Charley, where did you git yo' name?
Why, from takin' all de centimes in de ole crap game.

How they did roll their eyes and shake their supple bodies to the rhythm of that tune! The accompanist had been "piped down"—the singers had lost their self-consciousness. They began to loosen up and really sing. The piano droned a plaintive repetition of fifths that made an admirable background for the voices. The speed of the tune increased. The refrains were sung more softly.

Service record's gone, sure 'nuff—
Come on, bones, and treat me nice.
Phœbe, Phœbe, do your stuff—
Roll 'em, soldier, roll dose dice.

O, crap-shootin' Charley, where did you git your name?
Why, from takin' all de centimes in de ole crap game.
Crap-shootin' Charley, where did you git your name?
Why, from takin' all de centimes in de ole crap game.

The drumming of the piano became less like music. It was a throbbing something that seemed to mark out the rhythmic pattern on which the tune was hung. I was reminded of the crap-shooting performances of the past—the Issoudun crap games—ten thousand francs on the floor at one time—

men fading one another for piles of uncounted one and two franc paper bills; crap games back in Kentucky—on court days—on election days—on the guard decks of steamboats —in the shade of a pile of merchandise on the levee.

The fire had burned low. I began to be terribly homesick. The recurring fifths in the accompaniment were getting under my skin.

> Lost my hind leg in a poker game—
> Come on, bones, and treat me nice.
> Pasteboard gamblin's too damn tame—
> Roll 'em, soldier, roll dose dice.

The effect was intended to be humorous.

> Have to make dat awful box-car point—
> Come on, bones, and treat me nice.
> If de freights don't soon ride, I'll clean out dis joint—
> Roll 'em, soldier, roll dose dice.

The fire burned very low. I heard the music through drowsy ears. A strange sense of detachment came over me. I was a little boy again in a straw jimmie hat and bare feet. My father and I were in the Lee Line Steamboat offices. He held me by the hand. Men in broad black hats and moustaches were talking about McKinley, Bryan, Coxie's army. Robert, the colored boy who brushed out and shined the cuspidors, was showing me how to make a line fast to a Junie bug's leg. The bug escaped us. Robert spat into his hand and struck the spittle with his black forefinger, so that the path of the spittle might direct us in discovering the lost bug. McKinley—Bryan—free silver—Coxie's army—my father—the levee with its endless piles of merchandise—the lost Junie bug. Was I homesick!

> Crap-shootin' Charley, where did you git your name?
> Why, from takin' all de centimes in de ole crap game.

CRAP–SHOOTIN' CHARLEY

Arranged by J. J. N.

Verse

All I needs is twenty francs, Come on, bones, and treat me nice. Oh

pa - pa's look - in' for a nat-ural; Roll 'em, sol - dier, roll dose dice.

(A shout from the boys, and then the chorus.)

Chorus

Crap - shoot - in' Char - ley, where did you get your name? Why, from

tak - in' all de cen - times in de ole crap game.

Next day (another one of those soggy fall days when we couldn't see the "wind sock" for the fog), I had mess with some of the officers of the labor battalion. They had told me of a working-song their boys sang (somehow, they seemed to know that I was keeping a diary of soldier music). The mess was excellent. One of their cooks had been a chef in an American dining-car. Later I listened in on the working-song. Through a copying of notes I have lost the music to the verses. Otherwise the song is quite complete. The chief singer proved to be "Mr. Mooney Dukes," the soloist of the night before. He swung a pick and sang in the exact rhythm of his bodily movements.

> Diggin', diggin', diggin' in Kentucky—
> Diggin' in Tennessee; diggin' in North Carolina—
> Diggin' in France.

There were six measures of music to the refrains. Of the many verses Mooney sang, I have recorded only three.

> Slumgullion in de oven—
> Coffee in de pot—
> Snap yourself up into line
> An' git it while it's hot.
>   (*Diggin'*, etc.)

THE MIGHTY MOONEY WITH HIS PICK

Sharpen up my shovel,
And shine up my pick,
'Cause I can't scratch dis hard cold ground
Wid a crooked stick.
   (*Diggin'*, *etc.*)

Motor trucks and caissons
Cut a mighty trench,
Have to pile de metal on
Fur dese poor damn French.
   (*Diggin'*, *etc.*)

DIGGIN'

ARRANGED BY J. J. N.

Dig - gin',   dig - gin',   dig - gin' in Ken - tuc - ky;

Dig - gin'   in   Ten - nes - see;   Dig - gin'   in

Mis - sis - sip - pi;   Dig - gin'   in   France.

According to certain faded notes in my diary, Minnie May was a scarlet woman. Her scarletry was best known in the fair, sunny city of Natchez, Mississippi. She was one of those long, tall, brown-skinned gals who make preachers lay their Bibles down. Her meteoric career was brief—Abner cut her down—right to size. All that remained to make the job complete was the recountal by an American negro stevedore on the docks at St. Nazaire. The singer accompanied himself, playing a banjo-uke (supplied by one of the more philanthropic welfare organizations).

A troopship named *The Finland* had just landed. Stevedores swarmed over her like flies. They toted boxes, bags, bundles, and steel rails. Night came on. Shifts changed. They were now lifting net-loads of company baggage over the side. One net gave way just as it began to move over the narrow strip of water to the dock. Foot-lockers hit the water with a hollow, sounding splash. A second lieutenant, who had not soldiered enough to know the way of war, had been kicking around in the hold of *The Finland*, looking for the very baggage that had just gone over the side.

"You mean to tell me that when the net broke, you made no effort to recover the lost articles? Why, goddamit, everything I own was in my foot-locker—everything I own!"

"Don't think it matters much, Mr. Lieutenant. Course we is powerful sorry—but can't nothin' be done."

"Well, I'm a son of a sea cook, how's that for guts! Drop your baggage over and proceed to tell you that it's just too bad. Didn't you do anything?"

"Yassar, we done somethin'. We yelled 'jump from under,' but it didn't do no good—waren't nobody under jus' then. Course, de reason why we says it don't matter much 'bout your traps, is cause de colonel's baggage wuz los' too."

In the early days of the war, the French used many German prisoners on and about the docks at St. Nazaire. A small barracks had been built near the most important centre of shipping, where the Germans used to stay while on the water-front detail. Although it had to be removed as an obstacle to the tremendous operations of 1918, it was used a short while by some special details of American negro stevedores. Here they used to loaf while off duty. An improvised canteen had been established in one end. Here it was that a rather sawed-off sooty black boy from Natchez, Mississippi, sang the sad story of Minnie May. He was a blubber-lipped lad, mouthing his words in a grotesque manner, and rolling his eyes in wide circles to emphasize the moral of his yarn. His performance was an imitation of a Natchez street-singer, who practised mendicancy and religion for whatever living he gained. The song was sung to the tune of "Ashes to Ashes, Dust to Dust."

GERMAN PRISONERS

> Oh, I know a tale about a young high brown,
> Who vamped every man in her home town.
> > (*Here follows the usual two-line chorus.*)
>
> Now dis brown skin's name wuz Minnie May—
> She wore a purple kimona most every day.
> > (*Chorus.*)

She had money in 'er stockin's and earrings in 'er ears—
But 'bout de Day of Judgment she had some fears.
(*Chorus.*)

Now Minnie May cut a swath that wuz wide and deep—
But a sergeant-major named Abner—he put 'er to sleep.
(*Chorus.*)

De way she vamped dat soldier boy was an honest shame—
Folks said he couldn't even remember 'is name.
(*Chorus.*)

Now Abner didn't mind dat gal rompin' aroun'
But when she played 'im double, he put 'er under de
groun'.   (*Chorus.*)

De brethren and de sisters stood around and prayed,
But de debil's price, it had to be paid.
(*Chorus.*)

Now all o' you gals wid fire in your blood,
You better be sure my story's understood.
(*Chorus.*)

When Gabriel blows his bugle call,
You're goin' to have to confess your sins an' all.
(*Chorus.*)

Now drop your change right in de plate—
An' be sorry for your sins before it's too late.
(*Chorus.*)

* * *

One day in September, the A. P. M. at the Toul Railway
Station overhauled me with a sheaf of orders. I had done
some rather crazy flying during the forenoon. Among other
things, I had nearly hit another ship as I landed on the
Collombey les Belles field—a ship with two officers in it and
two mechanics in front of it. The A. P. M. brassard and the
sheaf of orders gave me a scare for a moment, but my fears

were quickly quieted. The military police officer wanted to intercept any one of a dozen pilots who were supposed to pass through the station that afternoon and send him to Vinets instead of Orly. A side-car was outside waiting to make the trip. There were a number of ships at the Vinets field ready to be delivered to the fighting squadrons with the least possible delay.

For some reason (I can no longer remember), we went by way of Bar le Duc and St. Dizier. It was one of those intoxicating fall days—scattered groups of white mare's tails spun lightly across the sky. Looking off through wooded sections of countryside, one saw the faint suggestion of a purple haze. It would soon be autumn. Already there were swirls of withered leaves in the fence corners and the gullies beside the roads. Off to the right we could see the observation balloons—a few swinging with the full play of their cables; others, part of the way out. The Boche had no doubt shot down some of our observers—the others were being kept within easy "hauling-in" reach. Just beyond Bar le Duc we encountered a very bad stretch of highway. My side-car driver suggested that we try another road. At the next intersection some M. P.'s were carrying on a bantering conversation.

"Why—why, Mogul, I hardly organized you. All reared back wid a M. P. badge on. Why ain't you up where de war is?"

"Oh, I'se detailed here on M. P. duty."

"You's yellow. You got S-O-S-itis, I know."

"No, boy, I ain't yellow; I wuz put here, honest. I has to pick up stragglers."

"Star Spangled Banner'll be sung fo' you in 'bout one minute. You, all reared back doin' M. P. duty. Might jus' ez well unrear yourself and straggle up to where de war is. Back areas is only fo' sick folks an' Tin Hat Generals."

"Say, you're talkin' right big, ain't you? How'd *you* git here, anyway?"

MOGUL HAD S–O–S–ITIS

"Me? Oh, I'se a walkin' case. I wuz ridin' on de front of a ambulance and when I got off, dey went off an' left me. I'll grab another 'fore long."

"You a walkin' case. Walkin' fo' what?"

"Shot in de ear, can't you see?"

"What I wants to see is your tags. Never wuz such a army as de Germans to be always shootin' folks in de ears! Why not shoot a few o' you all straight on—have it over."

"Listen, brother, it's all over as fur as I can tell. I'm goin' to put in fo' M. P. duty when my ear gits O. K."

I thought I had listened to enough of their smart talk.

"Will one of you boys take time out long enough to tell me about the road to St. Dizier?"

Mogul took me very seriously.

"Yassar, yassar, right now, sir."

"Well, what I want to know is this—is there another road to St. Dizier, and if so, where is it?"

"Well sir, no sir. They ain't but one fur sure and one that's kind of a country lane. Now, down here where you sees Christ in the Sentry Box, de bumps wears out—after that, you has smooth sailin'. Just turn to de right down yonder at Christ in the Sentry Box, yessar, it's a fair road from there on."

The road was well marked on the map, but the map had not been in the war as long as the road had.

"Sorry to jounce you 'round so, lieutenant," said Prince, the driver of my side-car. "Engineers ain't done much to improve dis mud hole."

Burlap bags (originally intended to be filled with earth and used for gun emplacements and trench constructions) had been loaded with the remains of stone buildings and piled side by side, making the most perfect of corduroy roads —every bag a bump. Just then we passed the roadside shrine, which had been referred to as "Christ in the Sentry Box," turned to the right, and sure enough, it was a very fair road. The little town of Wassy would be our first stop. We would try to make it in time for the evening meal. I had some very pleasant memories of other dinners at the Wassy Hotel—the marvellous meat-pies—the roast duck, the jams and jellies made after the Bar le Duc formula.

It was growing dark when we entered the Val Forest just beyond St. Dizier. The mellow odor of late September was in the air. There were no stars. Now and then we passed timid groups of faintly lighted buildings—buildings that had the theatrical air of unreality about them. Prince stopped to tinker with the engine. As long as the motor turned over, the cheerful noise of the exhaust had kept me from hearing the thick-set silence of the forests. It was unbelievably still. The trees almost met overhead.

"Having trouble, Prince?"

"Nossar, only a nut on my spark control jiggles loose. I didn't want to lose it."

Rain fell—at first, lightly—seeming to try our willingness to be drenched. Just as we were entering the village of Attancourt, I heard a banging noise. Prince stopped suddenly. We had hit one too many bumps. A rod connecting the side-car to the motorcycle had broken off.

"An', lieutenant, de skies is comin' down. "We're goin' to git ourselves soaked—we is, for sure."

The disabled motorcycle was rolled under the shelter of a wagon-yard. A local mechanic examined the breakage and said he would patch up the side-car so we might at least make the remaining four kilometres to Wassy.

"I had a feelin' de skies would come down. I gits it from my daddy to tell signs o' weather. He always told farmers when to plant crops fur above and when to plant fur below. Course he ain't got no chance to talk to farmers much now, 'cause he's in Chicago—in my home in Chicago."

It was raining steadily. The local mechanic fumbled

around in the semi-darkness, making very little progress. I suspected that Prince's father might prove interesting. At least, Prince wanted to talk to some one. I relaxed and listened.

"Nossar, my daddy don't care so much fo' Chicago. He's sixty year old now. Chicago is fur new style colored folks. We used to live 'bout five mile from Macon, Georgia. We owned a little general store. My daddy preached de Baptist religion on de side. You has colored folks about you callin' 'emselves 'hardshell Baptists,' ain't you, lieutenant?"

"Yes, lots of them, and whites, too."

"Yassar. In big meetin's, when we had lots o' jiners, my daddy could speak de 'unknown tongue.' Oh, yassar, he wuz a powerful singer. Never failed to have jiners when he'd sing

'I don't want to go till I puts my hand in his'n.'"

I began to be glad the side-car had broken down. Prince was full of his tale. I encouraged him to give the details.

"My daddy had been prayin' for a long time so his congregation might have a new church house. The brethren and de sisters made up a rule so as each of 'em would bring a brick every time they'd come to meetin'. Didn't matter much what kind o' brick it was, so long as it was a brick. We had a passel o' brick—Pavin' brick, Face brick, Fire brick, Enamel'd brick—

"All ready to be sot into a church house. One day a new-fangled preacher come to our diggin's. Preached in a tent. My daddy's congregation fell off. He prayed about it. He asked God to make him a sign. Nex' come Wednesday night when dis here new-fangled preacher was a carryin' on in his tent, a storm come along. Lightnin' struck his tent. Waren't no more tent. Waren't no more new-fangled preachin'. My daddy said God had spoke his mind. Folks said my daddy had put a curse on dis new-fangled preacher. . . . I went to Chicago 'bout dat time. In a little while, my daddy sold his store and come to Chicago, too. He couldn't preach no more in Georgia. Folks said he was a witch, 'count of de lightnin' strikin' de camp meetin'. Funny how both preachers wuz gone. But dey is a mighty pile of unsot brick in Georgia—My daddy's monument. Face brick, Pavin' brick, Fire brick, All kinds o' brick—A mighty pile of unsot brick—My daddy's monument in Georgia."

It was late when we finally arrived at Wassy, but in my notes I had a record of the song that "never failed to bring jiners" to the altar rail of the little church in Georgia. It was a plaintive, tuneless affair, invented, no doubt, by the old negro himself.

I have often wondered what that French mechanic made of my writing down the song, stopping Prince now and again, asking him to repeat a passage several times until I could grasp the tone picture and the rhythmic pattern of the music. There is a mighty pile of unset bricks in Georgia—Face bricks, Paving bricks, Fire bricks, Enamelled bricks—But it seems that the most enduring monument Prince's father could ever have will be the record of two noble songs his

war - rior in de ar - my of de Lord............

Verse

My God is a might - y God in bat - tle......

My God is a vic-tor in de fight. My God is a

might-y God in bat - tle; He's fight-in' for de right.

son passed on to me—"I Don't Want to Go," recorded in Attancourt, and "I'm a Warrior," recorded later.

I'M A WARRIOR

Oh, I'm a warrior in de army—
I'm a warrior for de Lord,
Oh, I'm a warrior,
I'm a warrior in de army of de Lord.

My God is a mighty God in battle—
My God is a victor in de fight—
My God is a mighty God in battle—
He's fightin' for de right.

Oh, I'm a sojer in de army—
I'm a sojer for de Lord,
I'm a sojer,
I'm a sojer in de army of de Lord.

ARRANGED BY J. J. N.

Oh, I don't want to go. Oh, I don't want to go. Oh, I don't want to go, till I puts my hand in his'n. Oh, Prom-ise ob sal-va-tion. Oh,

Prom - ise ob sal - va - - - - - tion. Oh, Prom - ise ob sal -

va - - tion, won't you set me free?

I Don't Want to Go

Oh, I don't want to go—
I don't want to go—
Oh, I don't want to go—
Till I puts my hand in his'n.

Oh, promise of salvation—
Promise of salvation—
Promise of salvation—
Won't you set me free?

Oh, bloody cross of Jesus—
Bloody cross of Jesus—
Bloody cross of Jesus,
Won't you set me free?

Oh, holy tongues of fire—
Holy tongues of fire—
Holy tongues of fire—
Won't you set me free?

Oh, mighty draught of fishes—
Mighty draught of fishes—
Oh, mighty draught of fishes—
Won't you set me free?

Oh, promise over Jordan—
Promise over Jordan—
Oh, promise over Jordan—
Won't you set me free?

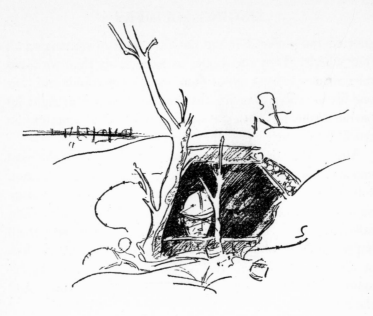

CHAPTER III

LIGHTS were never displayed on those roads around Toul
or Bar-le-Duc in the fall of 1918. . . . The drivers of
army motor vehicles were said to be "ambigodamdex-
trous" and knew the roads besides, while the hapless passen-
gers smoked, took swigs at straw-covered bottles, fondled
lucky pieces, and wished.

The particular motor vehicle we were riding in—known
to army folks as a camion—had the word "Fiat" stamped
on the side of it. It was inclined to be weak on the hills, but
possessed of unbelievable speed on the level stretches. We
passed the usual collection of staff cars, going hell-bent-for-
breakfast, some heavily laden Q. M. trucks, and then an all-
metal ammunition train. . . .

The ammunition trucks were slow-going devices—they

snorted and puffed, but had the advantage of steering on all four wheels. They could miss us more easily than we could miss them—at least, all of them except one could, and that one hit us a jolt that put the radiator of our Fiat right up on the dashboard with the steering-post. That ammunition truck didn't even stop—they were so sturdy. . . .

After the crash our Fiat staggered to the edge of the road and slid down a grassy embankment, where it turned bottom side uppermost in about six inches of stagnant water—stagnant water, green water, and mud. . . . The men who could talk the loudest tried to explain to one another how it all happened; the others felt their bodies for any possible loss or damage, extricating themselves the while from the remains of the Fiat, the foot-lockers, the musette bags, and the map cases. . . .

Some time later a Quartermaster truck kindly took part of us aboard. The fact that the truck was headed in the general direction of our original destination (the railway station at Toul) assured us at least that we were on our way. . . .

The city of Toul dates back to Roman times. It boasts of a wall, a moat, and a practical drawbridge. These relics of antique warfare might have assured some of the more trusting citizenry, but soldiers merely smiled when they thought of the sturdy drawbridge under a salvo of 42 c. m. howitzers. The 42 c. m. howitzers were held off, however, through the fortunate existence of a chain of defenses (known as the Toul-Nancy Defense System), designed and brought to a fair state of completion in the spring of 1914 by one Ferdinand Foch, soldier extraordinaire. . . .

The Q. M. truck dropped us off on the south side of the city near a huge pile of army material. . . . One thing par-

ticularly attracted our attention—coils of smooth iron wire.
. . . The wire was piled under a grove of trees, like a great
heap of black doughnuts. . . . Strange to say, this wire
was still there under the same trees long after the Armistice
was signed—it had never been used. . . . We were later
told by a member of the French Engineers that the wire had

undoubtedly been intended to reinforce concrete pill-box
forts for the additional protection of the Toul-Nancy sector
. . . but as the centre of the war moved northward, the
idea had been abandoned. . . .

There were other Q. M. trucks besides the one we had
ridden in—they were being loaded and unloaded by gangs
of colored boys. Some of the boys sang as they worked. . . .

Black man fights wid de shovel and de pick—
Lordy, turn your face on me—

LORDY, TURN YOUR FACE

Arranged by J. J. N.

Black man fights wid de shov-el and de / pick;

Lord-y, turn your face on me. Nev-er gits no rest 'cause he

nev-er gits sick; Lord-y, turn your face on me.

He never gits no rest 'cause he never gits sick . . .
Lordy, turn your face on me. . . .

These colored boys had not seen actual fighting. . . .
They had been detailed to a less glorious, but by no means
less important side of warfare. . . . The first and third lines
were sung by a single voice, while the second and fourth
were sung in a freely harmonized manner by all who wished
to join in. . . . Many times this ensemble singing was almost lost in the noise of the moving feet and the picking up
and putting down of heavy objects. . . . It was more like
an echo. . . .

> Jined de army fur to git free clothes—
> Lordy, turn your face on me—
> What we're fightin' 'bout, nobody knows—
> Lordy, turn your face on me. . . .

As we look back on the results of the war, we are prone to
think that this verse was composed by a philosopher, indeed. . . .

> Never goin' to ride dat ocean no more—
> Lordy, turn your face on me—
> Goin' to walk right home to my cabin door . . .
> Lordy, turn your face on me.* . . .

* This last verse reminds one of the tale told by an American officer who returned
to France after an absence of two years. One day while travelling through one of
the areas occupied by American troops during the war, he happened to see a colored
fellow wearing a very tattered suit of clothes, part of which proved to be American
issue olive drab. After much questioning, the colored man gave up his pose and
confessed himself to be an American soldier who had deserted rather than go home
on a ship. "Yes, sar," he said, "I knows I'se a deserter. I knows they has a place
made special fur me at Levensworth—I knows—but even so, I ain't goin' to ride
dat ocean. No, sar! An' if ever dey do come atter me in sich numbers as I sees
I must go home, den by gollies, I'll jus' walk home if I has to go 'round by way
o' New Orleans. . . ."

We thought how often in the production of the drama, theatrical producers and managers had unsuccessfully tried to gain the very effect we beheld at that moment. . . . The faces of the singers could not be seen. . . . To us they were only black masses moving in the rhythm of a song—a song admirably revealing an indomitable spirit of philosophic humor, which has survived so many generations of suppression. . . .

As we turned to go, we realized that the camion accident had caused us to miss the only fast train for many hours. . . . We no longer had any reason to hurry. The air of the early fall night blew softly against our faces as we wearily followed the Toul wall around to the most eastern side, where the railway station was. The road passed immediately beside one of the many branches of the Moselle-Rhine canal system. Peak-roofed barges were huddled at the canal sides—clusters of miniature Noah's Arks, weathered almost black from uncounted years of exposure, seeming to gain courage through numbers. At one place we encountered some lock tenders allowing the passage of a tow. . . . They sang bits of a laboring song at one another, employing an almost incomprehensible jargon of French patois. . . .

Farther off to the right we could see the trees that skirted the Moselle—the Moselle on its way to Metz and, farther on, into the Rhine. . . . Left of us lay the city—ever so quietly—as if it were holding its breath lest some one find it out. . . . A church tower or more imposing building occasionally raising its head above the edge of the wall and the thick black mantle of trees. . . .

What battles had been fought and might be fought again upon the very ground we trod! We looked to the northeast.

The sky was streaked with orange and red. The air trembled a bit. A battery of long-range guns firing its nightly ration of shells brought us back from the days of Jeanne d'Arc to our own tragically unromantic war. . . .

In the space before the railway station the Red Cross Canteen was doing capacity business. Almost every Allied uniform was represented in the two long lines which crept slowly, endlessly into the hut. The canteen workers were not as spick and span as usual. They were very weary. They no longer resembled the Red Cross girls found on posters back in the States. They had been on the job since early morning. In the past two weeks they had had little or no rest. For there was a war going on just over the way. Troops seemed to be coming from everywhere.

One of the lines coming into the hut had halted. Four boys were carrying on a whispered conversation with the girl behind the counter.

"Listen, miss, we only got about sixty centimes between us. Could you fix us up on a little something? We're sure hungry. Here it is—it's sixty-five centimes."

The chocolate, tea, or coffee with sandwiches served was usually ten to fifteen centimes. Their pooled resources might have paid the bill. But there was a war going on just over yonder. There had been a jolly bombing raid earlier in the evening—part of the station near by had been smashed in. . . . What was sixty centimes to the Red Cross Canteen at Toul! Cups of something hot and a sandwich each were pushed over the counter to them. Their sixty centimes were also pushed over to them. . . .

"Come around after a while and help me cut some bread, or—let's see, maybe you can wash a few cups. Keep the centimes—you may need 'em."

They gulped their food in silence. It must be true, then. These Janes from America could be kind to buck privates— they were not all given to specializing on gold oak-leaves and silver eagles. The lad with the remains of an ugly cut on his forehead spoke first.

"Goddam if I ever had it happen to me before. An' she's

a Jew. Sonovabitch if I don't wash cups. I'll wash the whole bloody godamn canteen. An' she even give us back our centimes. Never had it happen before."

The others had no words. They looked dumbly at the Jewess, whose lovely brown eyes smiled a recognition to each boy as he took his food and gave way to the next . . . smiled as nearly as her weariness would permit.

We knew her well. She had been at our camp in Issoudun early in the war. We talked over old times—Issoudun—

"the muddiest hole in all France." The wild New Year's shooting match. Our camp newspaper, now the highly organized *Plane News*. She called us by our first names. Indeed, we were regarded with suspicion by the long lines that crept —slowly—endlessly—into the hut.

Back stage, in the canteen's kitchen, I found a very particular friend of mine—a Red Cross girl from St. Louis. She had four colored boys helping her with a pot-washing job. They were from one of the infantry regiments of the 92d Division, then passing through Toul—riding in the side-door Pullmans Française—forty to the car.

As I elaborated on the "Lordy, Turn Your Face On Me" working-song, singing to my St. Louis friend snatches of the tune, I noticed one of the colored boys getting his mouth made up for a speech.

"Please, sar . . . would de flyin' machine lieutenant like to hear our song 'bout de French railway man?"

For the next five minutes the Red Cross pots were scoured to the rhythm of the French railway song. The verses were almost tuneless. I was too sleepy to struggle with writing it down. I did, however, scratch off the tune of the chorus. The verses were sung to four measures of music, but the chorus made up the unusual number of ten measures, and the words required the use of the word "Bush" (meaning Boche) to rhyme with the word "push." Altogether the song was a delicious piece of reckless, errant imagination.

Oh, you jined up fur fightin' in a he-man's war.
An' you're goin' to do your fightin' in a French freight car.

Chorus:
Oh, mister French railroad man, whar you takin' us to—
Please, mister French railroad man, whar you takin' us to—

Goin' to take you up fo' de next big push—
Goin' to let you take a swing at dose awful "Bush"*—
Oh, I knows dey's trouble ahead.

Ride all night and ride all day—
Got to stand up straight, 'cause dey's no place to lay.
(*Chorus.*)

Forty men and eight army horses—
Goin' to come back home wid some nice German crosses.
(*Chorus.*)

If I gits home to the land of de free—
Pullman train'll be the place for me.
(*Chorus.*)

Mr. Engineer, won't you please haul your freight,
My feet is singing a hymn of hate.
(*Chorus.*)

Oh, I knows dey's trouble up yonder ahead—
But it wouldn't matter much if I could lay my head.
(*Chorus.*)

God, how sleepy I was. For two nights and two days we
had been either flying or bumping over the French country-

---

* The use of the word "Bush" in the French Railroad Man Song brings to mind
the following yarn—related to me by one of the negro boys who had seen service
on the front—he was describing the fighting qualities of the various armies. . . .
"Now boy, dis here French army is a whale of a fightin' machine. . . . Dey has
all de trick affairs for makin' war . . . long range guns, grenades, and a passel of
inventions we ain't never heard of yit. . . . An' dose bayonets dey use—long ones,
three-cornered like a overgrown needle. . . . Yes, and dese English lads—wonderful fighters. . . . Dey drinks a lot of tea but dey does fight. . . . An' de Italians,
an' de Australians, *an'* de Belgians, *an'* de Germans wid dose machine guns dat
shoot so slow and go in so deep. . . . But Mister, let me tell you dis one thing
. . . if ever you have to go out yonder and have to fight in dis war like I did—
fight wid 'em—grapple wid 'em—stick at 'em wid bayonets—take my word for
de truth and look out for dose Bush—look out for dose Bush, dey is hell." . . .
(The story-teller thought the so-called Boche, mispronounced "Bush," were an
entirely different army.)

side in camions. My feet hung as if they were weighted.
I'd lost my equipment in the last camion smash. The other
members of the outfit envied my good fortune. I had nothing to carry—not even a map-case.

Once inside the railway station I wandered across the
tracks to the eastern end of the yard, where part of the

HOMMES 40—CHEVEAUX 8

366th Infantry Regiment of the 92d Division and a train-
load of French artillerymen were sidetracked. The Frenchmen had lashed their gun-carriages and caissons to the tops
of flat-cars. The barrels of the guns were pointed sharply
skyward—slender barrels of seventy-fives, poking through
tarpaulins, like the tail feathers of giant birds with their
heads under their wings, asleep in rows on flat-cars.

Both the colored boys of the 366th and the French artillerymen were riding "Hommes quarante—cheveaux huit."
The centres of the cars were piled high with equipment, the

men sprawling about in whatever unoccupied space they could find. Food was being passed out to the 366th.

"Fust time we has et in hell knows when."

"FUST TIME WE HAS ET IN HELL KNOWS WHEN"

Up toward the head end of the train they were singing. I debated with myself a long time before I mustered up enough energy even to go and listen. The song was too naïve to miss. I took down the words and later, in the office of the A. P. M., after one of my boys had given me a generous hooker of good hard rum, I wrote off what I could remember of the music. There seemed to be a difference of opinion about some of the lines in the refrain. One group of the colored boys sang about Mississippi—others referred to Tennessee. I assumed the Tennessee version to have more basis of fact—thereupon, it found a place in the manuscript.

It was a sleepy-eyed, muchly blotted manuscript, but I stuck to the task of writing it off, knowing that it would be a long while before I'd have the good fortune to encounter three original songs in one day.

German throwed a hand grenade—
Waren't no use 'cause its innards wuz dead. . . .
Good-by—I says good-by. . . .
Good-by—uhm hmm—
Good-by, Tennessee, twill I sees you again.

When 366 went over de top—
Kaiser's army wuz a flop. . . .
Good-by—I says good-by. . . .
Good-by—uhm hmm—
Good-by, Tennessee, twill I sees you again.

President said go git yo' gun—
Cause, Sam, you'll have to fight dat Hun. . . .
Good-by—I says good-by. . . .
Good-by—uhm hmm. . . .
Good-by, Tennessee, twill I sees you again.

Colonel says you'll have to plough
Trenches, 'cause dis war's a wow. . . .
Good-by—I says good-by. . . .
Good-by—uhm hmm. . . .
Good-by, Tennessee, twill I sees you again.

VERSE

The little responsive "uhm hmms" were either sung by some one near by or by the soloist himself. Once the assisting singer sang "I says good-by . . ." The form of the song varied with the verses. One might say that the singers defied form and note value in an attempt to gain an unusual rhythm and tell their story at the same time.

Doctor says you'd better take
Something 'long fur stomach-ache. . . .
Good-by—I says good-by—
Good-by—uhm hmm. . . .
Good-by, Tennessee, twill I sees you again.

Tote my rabbit's foot to charm
Hun, so's he can't do no harm. . . .
Good-by—I says good-by—
Good-by—uhm hmm. . . .
Good-by, Tennessee, twill I sees you again.

I knows a place in Tennessee—
Where fried spring chicken is a waitin' fur me. . . .
Good-by—I says good-by—
Good-by—uhm hmm. . . .
Good-by, Tennessee, twill I sees you again.

* * *

When all the saw-toothed bayonets and German helmets
have rusted into iron oxide, we will still have "Mademoiselle
from Armentiers" as one of the imperishable souvenirs of
this man's war. The negro boys I encountered were "off"
"Mademoiselle from Armentiers." It seemed that as they
had little to do with its manufacture, they would not adver-
tise it by singing it more than occasionally. In white outfits, however, one was sure to find a cook, a barracks orderly,
or a company jester, who would, with little or no encouragement, sing 391 verses of this epic. The verses varied with
the experiences and duty detail of the singer. Usually there
were but a few good verses, and several hundred where the
rhymes were forced and the references were made to local
unimportant persons. The five verses offered here were supplied me by a member of the 367th Infantry Regiment.
This regiment was known as "The Buffaloes."

The colored boys were sidetracked near the Bar le Duc Railway Station. The spokesman was contemptuous of replacements.

"We is members of de first batallion. We is Buffaloes—

GERMANS — MAKE PEACE
WITH YOUR GOD—ALABAMA
SOLDIERS · HAS GOT
YOU BY THE SEAT OF
YOUR PANTS

original Buffaloes. All de rest of dese here baboons you-all sees here-'n-abouts is only replacements."

Mademoiselle from Armentiers, parlez-vous,
Mademoiselle from Armentiers, parlez-vous,
I'se glad I is a Buffalo—
'Cause we is always on de go—
Inky dinky,* parlez-vous.

Mademoiselle from Armentiers, parlez-vous,
Mademoiselle from Armentiers, parlez-vous,

* The negro sang "Inky Dinky" rather than "Hinky Dinky."

I'd like to git myself a sip
O' what you got restin' on your hip—
Inky Dinky, parlez-vous.

Mademoiselle from Armentiers, parlez-vous,
Mademoiselle from Armentiers, parlez-vous,
I wouldn't give my high-brown belle,
For every mademoiselle dis side o' hell—
Inky Dinky, parlez-vous.

Mademoiselle from Armentiers, parlez-vous,
Mademoiselle from Armentiers, parlez-vous,
I can't read nor I can't write,
But, boy, when I has to, I can fight,
Inky Dinky, parlez-vous.

I don't know dis Mademoiselle from Armentiers,
I don't know dis Mademoiselle from Armentiers,
I don't know and I don't care,
Ef she was really ever there,
Inky Dinky, parlez-vous.

(*Diary note, Oct. 12, 1918.*) "*Landed in a funny little evacuation hospital just over the hill from Collombey les Belles, this morning. The Doc at camp said he didn't know whether I had a plain sore throat, flu, or spinal meningitis. The food is simply terrible—uncooked goldfish and raw onions for lunch —some diet for a sick man. And the coffee—wow! . . .*

(*October 13th.*) . . . *lots of shot-up lads in this shake-down —and some of the funniest orderlies I ever saw. The two in our ward are named "Pancho Pete" and "Bed Pan Bill." The black orderlies are much more interesting and what's more important, they sing. When they let me out I'll write some of their tunes down. . . .*

(*October 17th.*) . . . (*On the way to Toul*) *What a hospital that was. I've gone over the list and thanked all the gods, their assistants, the bishops, the saints, the rabbis, and the apostles*

*that I got out of that place alive. I'll never be able to look at a
raw onion again. Not a bad song though, these colored orderlies sang, about the 'Burden-Bearer'."*

When you feels dat you mus' go—weepin' days for Jesus,
Leave your burden here below—weepin' days for Jesus.

Chorus :

For he's a burden-bearer, a burden-bearer, a burden-bearer,
For he's a burden-bearer, a burden-bearer, a burden-bearer.

HE'S A BURDEN-BEARER

ARRANGED BY J. J. N.

When you feels dat you must go, Weep-in days for Je - sus; Leave your bur - den here be - low, Weep-in' days for Je - sus. For He's a burden-

bearer, a burden - bearer, a burden - bearer. For

He's...... a burden - bearer,...... a bur - den -

bear-er,.... a burden - bear-er.....

I done helt my head too high—weepin' days for Jesus,
Goin' to let my pride go by,—weepin' days for Jesus.
(*Chorus.*)

When he climbed up Calvary—weepin' days for Jesus,
Totin' his cross for you and me—weepin' days for Jesus.
(*Chorus.*)

Soldier stuck 'im in de side—weepin' days for Jesus,
Dat's de time our Saviour died—weepin' days for Jesus.
(*Chorus.*)

White folks laid 'im in dat tomb—weepin' days for Jesus,
Hoped he'd stay twill de clap of doom—weepin' days for
Jesus.
(*Chorus.*)

Three days passed and he war out—weepin' days for Jesus,
Warn't no reason den for doubt—weepin' days for Jesus.
(*Chorus.*)

This song was opened by one singing of the chorus. Oftentimes between verses the chorus was sung twice.

* * *

One frosty morning in October, 1918, I was given orders
to fly a new type Spad from Orly-Seine to Issoudun (the
third Aviation Instruction Centre). The major explained
that my ship contained a very expensive collection of photo-
graphic equipment, and intimated that I might either land
the Spad and the equipment safely at Issoudun, or never
return to Orly.

It was not like old times to get back to Issoudun. The
barracks had been equipped with running water and other
twentieth-century sanitary contraptions, very unlike those
we had lived with and learned to like, in the old days—the
early days of 1917. The original and best-looking Red Cross

girls were gone. The *Plane News* had graduated into a big city sheet with colored supplements. The camp swarmed with newly arrived American lieutenants, in conspicuously new olive drab—gold-bar lieutenants in bright yellow Sam Browne belts. They looked at me in my moleskin pants and flying-coat (both stained with the oil and grease of many flights) and wondered what army I belonged to.

I had originally intended to remain in camp over night, but the news of a big-calibre railway wreck came in from the near-by town of Chateauroux. My plans were changed at once. A detail of men from Issoudun had been sent to clear away, to help restore a very necessary piece of roadbed. On the pretext of spending the night in Chateauroux (in order to catch an early train next morning) I left camp, riding on a truck headed in the direction of the wreck. It was a truck of food-stuffs, intended to ration the wrecking crews. The forward end of the truck was loaded with hard bread—hard bread, beans, and "canned bill." Aft they had stowed four galvanized-iron cans of hot coffee. The truck was springless, the roads were rutted, and the driver drove like "hell beatin' tanbark."

It was about 11.30 when we arrived at the scene of the wreck. The bed of the truck leaked coffee like an immense sieve. Not more than a third of the original contents of the can remained. The dry rations forward were awash with tepid coffee. A sergeant balled hell out of the driver and turned to a waiting line of hungry men.

"This is a sorry lookin' goddam mess, but chow is chow, fellows, an' you can just thank Christ that some of it came in water-tight tins."

The white boys ate sullenly and threw themselves on the ground for a moment's rest before going back to the clearing away. Some colored soldiers who had been temporarily quartered near Chateauroux were also working on the wreck.

After they had eaten, they turned to kidding their officers by singing the "Pay Roll Song."

"Pay Roll Song," to the tune of "Marching through Georgia."

> All we do is sign the pay roll
> All we do is sign the pay roll
> All we do is sign the pay roll
>   but we never get a goddam cent . . . .

I felt sure that before the night was over they'd sing something worth writing down. They sang the "Pay Roll Song" as often as it would stand repetition, then after a short pause and several bad starts struck up an original version of a very familiar old song about going home. Sitting on the seat of the ration truck, I wrote off their jingles on every piece of paper available, and later accidentally dropped the entire record in a puddle of cold coffee on the truck floor.

Next morning in Chateauroux, after the early train had been safely missed, a clear copy was made of the carefully dried notes. There were only eleven verses of the song. If the paper had held out I might have had twenty. When white boys sang this tune, they borrowed their verses from the songs of other wars—for example:

> I gave myself to Uncle Sam—
> Now I'm not worth a good goddam—
> I don't want any more France. . . .
> Jesus, I want to go home.

But the colored fellows made up their own verses. . . .

> When I came over I was mama's pride and joy—
> Now I'm just one of the Hoy-Poloy. . . .
> I don't want any more France. . . .
> Jesus, I want to go home.

> When I gits a chance to do my stuff—
> I'll strangle some German twill he hollers "nuff"—
> I don't want any more France. . . .
> Jesus, I want to go home.

> I brought my razor from the other side. . . .
> An' I hopes to whet dat blade on de Kaiser's hide . . .
> I don't want any more France—
> Jesus, I want to go home.

> Dices don't love their papa no more—
> Since we left dat United shore—
> I don't want any more France—
> Jesus, I want to go home.

My gal up an' called my bluff—
An' brother, did I do my stuff—
I don't want any more France—
Jesus, I want to go home.

Officers, they live up on de hill—
We live down in de muck and de swill—
I don't want any more France—
Jesus, I want to go home.

I got a gal—her name is May—
She holds me tight mos' all o' de day—
I don't want any more France—
Jesus, I want to go home.

Pay day, won't you please come 'round—
I wants to take a trip to Chateauroux town—
I don't want any more France. . . .
Jesus, I want to go home.

Soldier boy, don't you miss your aim—
'Cause when Heinie gits yo' range, it's goin' to be a
          shame—
I don't want any more France—
Jesus, I want to go home.

Don't waste yo' time wonderin' if every shell's a dud—
'Cause it only takes one to curdle yo' blood—
I don't want any more France—
Jesus, I want to go home.

If you don't want yo' bones to be used fur fertilize—
Better sing out yo' prayers and don't tell God no lies—
I don't want any more France—
Jesus, I want to go home.

*   *   *

I DON'T WANT ANY MORE FRANCE

Arranged by J. J. N.

Gave my-self to Un-cle Sam, Now I'm not worth a good God damn. I don't want an - y more France;... Je - sus, I want to go home.

That American chaplain so well known and so much loved by the sick and wounded in one of the hospitals, used to swap with a colored boy a story for a song. The chaplain was an Irishman and, as one might expect, had an almost inexhaustible supply of tales. Some were more dry-cleaned than others, but every one, if properly told, carried a good legitimate laugh with it.

Prior to the war, the colored boy, affectionately called Bolo, had been employed in the turpentine forests of the Southland. From his songs and stories one gathered that the negroes of the turpentine country had developed an individual collection of "hants" and superstitions. His father, for example, had for many years been engaged in making and selling a so-called "voodoo-powder," which, when sprinkled across the doorways at night-time, was guaranteed to forestall the entrance of the dreaded needle-witch.*

Of the songs he sang, the one involving the moon was by far the most nearly unique. He said that the verses of this particular tune were part of the hymn tunes and shoutin' praise, used in his neck o' the woods back home, but he'd made up the chorus—modernized the text, one would say, to fit the idea of the war. (He called the choruses "The repeatin's"). Although both verses and tunes varied from time to time, the words were decidedly the most constant. . . .

> I don't think I'se long for here. . . .
> I seed a ring around de moon.
> I don't think I'se long for here. . . .
> An' de change can't come too soon.

---

*The needle-witch was a kind of harpy, who, after having been tarred and feathered by irate, upright citizens, during a long-ago witchcraft orgy, had wallowed herself in pine needles and appears thus to this very day, much resembling a porcupine.

Refrain:

Oh, stop up de mouths of dose cannons,
And throw yo' bayonets down. . . .
'Cause fightin' an' killin' ain't nothin' to do. . . .
When de day o' de Lord come around.

I don't know what's over dat hill. . . .
When dey's a ring around de moon. . . .
Want to go so bad I can't sit still. . . .
An' de goin' can't come too soon.
                    (*Refrain.*)

Done seed a angel in a dream. . . .
Dere wuz a ring around de moon. . . .
Said I'se goin' home in a cloud o' steam. . . .
An' it can't come true too soon.
                    (*Refrain.*)

Bolo had made the interesting error of assuming that any
bugle call which gave him a chance to stop work or drill,
making it possible for him to "rest his weary hips," was
Taps. He called it "The Sweet Ole Taps Tune." He even
sang a pathetic sort of song about it. It was the only practical musical thing he did. Both words and notes have been
recorded (the music to the "Moon Song" defied recording).

I'se goin' to lay myself right flat down,
Goin' to lay down an' sleep on de hard, cold ground—
I'se goin' to lay myself right flat down,
When I hears dat sweet ole Taps tune sound. . . .

Repeatin's:

For I'se weary,
Oh Jesus, so weary,
Sweet Jesus, so weary—

FOR I'SE WEARY

In body an' soul. . . .
I says I'se weary—
Oh Jesus, so weary,
Sweet Jesus, so weary—
In body an' soul. . . .

The so-called "repeatin's" gave the reason for the great desire to rest. . . .

When the United States Air Service purchased a supply
of Sopwith Camels from the English, we knew that it would
be up to us at Orly to fly them from the English airdromes
to our fields at Vinets and Collombey les Belles. The Camels
the English turned out were motored (as a rule) with French

Monosaupape rotary engines—very good engines when they didn't catch fire or fly to pieces from overheating. The success or failure of a pilot flying a Monosaupape Camel depended upon the pilot's knowledge of motors and delicacy of control. A Camel would do a loop, a hand stand, a vrille,

and a flop on the shortest notice of any machine we encountered (up to the end of the war) except perhaps the Moraine Monoplane. Many of our good boys died trying to fly Camels. They were tricky ships, particularly for the first few hops—after that, with any luck at all one could carry on quite safely. A few, who became quite expert with them, were jokingly referred to as "camel-drivers." One wild American at Vinets (a tester) used to take a Camel off the ground, go into a loop and land. Then he would take the ship off the ground in a chandelle, spiral upwards until he lost flying speed, kick over into a side slip and pull out just in time to save the bugler from blowing taps. We took this lad aside and, with tears in our eyes, convinced him that he was too valuable to the service to be such a deliberate and absolute ass. But, after all, the Camels were tricky air-ships.

It required both luck and technique to fly them and stay out of the graveyard.

When we "ferried" Camels from England to France, we went to Norwich (one of the English supply stations for aeronautical gear), by way of Paris, Le Havre, Southampton, and London. We had to stop in London long enough to report to the Royal Flying-Corps Air Pool for orders and collect a few pounds sterling in lieu of railroad fare from the American Q. M. This required about two days. We always made the most of these two-day stop-overs. On one of them we made the acquaintance of Lady Astor and her sister. They were originally from Virginia and very sympathetic with the South. We talked about Richmond, Virginia, and Lexington, Kentucky, the horse-races at Churchill Downs, the Derby at Louisville. I happened to have two boxes of loaf-sugar in my musette bag. Lady Astor's family had used saccharine for so long, they were most awfully pleased with the sugar. Next morning four American officers were invited to Buckingham Palace, where His Majesty the King pinned decorations on the breasts of soldiers. Now and then the soldier couldn't walk, and sometimes an empty coat-sleeve answered the King's salute. Later the American officers were presented to His Majesty and were so graciously received that they came away with a more kindly feeling toward the "divine right of kings." All of this in Buckingham Palace. At tea-time we sat around a fire in St. James Square. The hostess and her sister sweetened the tea with loaf-sugar out of my musette bag.

Across the street from the Astor Town House the British had constructed some temporary barracks—an officers' club —built around the equestrian statue of some one. It was here that we encountered an English pilot named Christy, who had originally been attached to a flying-outfit on the Italian frontier. His outfit, as I remember, was equipped with Bristols. Christy had been a newspaper man before the war. His knowledge of copy values had given him the idea of writing a book on "flying-soldiers"—he said he's read enough bad aviation tales. He felt it was high time for some one who knew the air and the job at which pilots lived and died, to belie the synthetically concocted claptrap we encountered on every hand.

It seems that Christy was in love with one of the young ladies who had volunteered to wait on tables at the Officers' Club in St. James Square. How charming a person she was and how unused to carrying heavy trays of dishes! She was naturally interested in Christy's book—he had promised to let her read the chapters as fast as he found time to turn them off. When we left next afternoon to go up to Norwich, Christy's sweetheart came to see us take our leave. Her violet eyes were misted from having just shed tears. They were very much in love, those two!—not as soldiers and war-workers loved, as a rule, but in a sincere, almost old-fashioned manner. Christy assured her he would fly carefully—not low and slow, but high and fast, and wait for good weather to make a Channel crossing.

"If you'll be a really good little girl, I'll bring you a surprise from Marquise."

"What, beside yourself?"

"Why, the first chapter of the book, of course."

My orders said that I would fly from Norwich to an American field in France, by way of Lympne and Marquise. Christy's orders took him as far as Marquise, the first landing-field on the French side of the Channel. We made the trip together from Norwich to Lympne, where we spent the night at the Officers' Club, in the twelfth-century castle restored by Beecham, the pill-maker. Next day we started across the Channel—it was a stormy flight—several ships turned back. With my usual luck I landed top side up at Marquise and waited at the pilotage for Christy.

They gave him up as missing in the early afternoon. By nightfall a driving rain had turned Marquise into the most dismal camp in France. I remembered some lines from Alan Seeger's poem, about being

"Pillowed in silk and scented down—
Where love throbs out in blissful sleep."

And then I thought of Christy—lost in the English Channel.

I shall always remember how much opposed he was to wearing life-belts, and thank myself for having strapped one on him ere I took off for Marquise. What his book would have been like no one will ever know—for though His Majesty paid a royal wage in ribbons, orders, and honors, neither the King nor his horses nor all of his men knew the pattern of Christy's book. That's why his sweetheart waited so long for that first chapter from Marquise.

Late next afternoon some ambulance-men extricated me from the remains of my plane. I had fallen in a lonesome little gully, not fifteen minutes' flight from my destination. Lady Luck had been played too hard. Up to that time I hadn't broken a wire or scratched a bit of wing covering. My memory is not clear on what happened during the next five semiconscious days, and I kept no diary. They were days of falling through space—grinding motors—barking archies—the storm-lashed English Channel—trying to fly through fog clouds—smashing struts—the ripping of wing-covering. Then out of all this chaos came voices speaking the English language—in an American manner. I was in the 45th Red Cross Hospital, St. Denis, France. A colonel of the Medical Corps was there, several other officers, a Red Cross nurse, and a negro orderly. My orderly's name was William. We were Southerners—he was a long, lanky North Carolinian—I was a Kentuckian.

William was the most picturesque liar I have ever known. What tales he told of his exploits in the army—the training-camps in France and America—of the troop-ships—the submarines—of North Carolina—and of his rabbit-foot method of recovery from shrapnel and mustard gas.

In addition to his charm as a prevaricator, he spoke in a dialect I had never before encountered. His overcoat was known as "ma objercoat"—he said "gart" for got, "poot" for put, "mought" for might, and "pite nye" for pretty nearly. He had an absolute mania for face-lotions, hair-tonics, perfumes, soaps, and powders, uniquely classifying such preparations as "scent-waters, love-powders, and hair-oils." He rather objected to the French hair-tonics, however, saying that they were too thin to make his wool stay put and would not shine shoes like the "burgmont" oil he had used in North Carolina.

The French Government had permitted the U. S. Army to house the 45th Red Cross Hospital in a school, built by Napoleon Premier, originally intended for the daughters of men who had been awarded the Legion of Honor. Left of the main building stood the Cathedral of St. Denis, a romantic old pile of Gothic architecture, in which many of the kings and queens of France are buried, and on the altar of which Joan of Arc in 1429 hung her white armor and the sword she had worn in so many victories.

There were 3,000 men in the 45th Red Cross Hospital

(this number was not furnished by William), and the memories of their suffering through those terrible days and nights are too sacred to recount. I do not know what I should have done without William.

Mine was a tiny room—a room with a fireplace in it. William sat Uncle-Remus-like, with his back to me, telling his stories into the fire. Between the telling of the fabulous yarns, William would sing. It wasn't exactly singing—it was more like crooning. It was the legend of a suppressed race of black men, whispered to an obligato of unbelievably fervent music—music that made me hold my breath, lest I should lose the very smallest part. It was easy to record

OLE ARK

De ole ark's a mov-er-in', a mov-er-in', a mov-er-in'; De ole ark's a mov-er-in, watch 'er go. De ole ark's a mov-er-in', mov-er-in', a mov-er-in','Cause Captain No-ah tole me so. Sol' my ma-my down at New Or-leans, Now we got to cook our own ham and greens. Oh, de ole ark's a mov-er-in', etc.

William's songs—he sang them so often I knew them by
heart. His version of "De Ole Ark's a Moverin'" was
unique, involving a conversation with Captain Noah.

> Oh, de ole ark's a moverin', a moverin', a moverin',
> De ole ark's a moverin'—watch 'er go.
> De ole ark's a moverin', a moverin', a moverin',
> 'Cause Captain Noah tole me so.
>
> Sol' my mammy down at New Orleans,
> Now we got to cook our own ham and greens.
> *(Oh, de ole ark's a moverin', etc.)*
>
> Sister, you bes' change your mind—
> Hell's a creepin' up on you from behind.
> *(Oh, de ole ark's a moverin', etc.)*
>
> Save a seat for me inside—
> 'Cause Noah knows I'se goin' to ride.
> *(Oh, de ole ark's a moverin', etc.)*

The usual expression of infinite faith found its way into
all of William's songs. He knew the more morbid of the
traditional negro tunes, but for some reason he avoided
them; perhaps in his childish way he knew that if faith
could move mountains, it could also heal wounded aviators
more easily than sour faces, potions, incantations, and hyp-
notic passes.

It's all very well for "all o' God's chillun" to have wings,
shoes, robes, crowns, etc., and to dance all over heaven thus
attired, but William sang a song about *being* "one of God's
chillun"—a song that had more fundamental religious phi-
losophy in it per line than many preachments have in them
per thousand words. He called it "The Gimmie Song."

GIMMIE SONG

ARRANGED BY J. J. N.

Verse

I knows I'se one ob God's chill - un,   an' he's goin' to gim-mie

what I needs. I knows I'se one ob de se - lect e - lect,

one ob de chill - un God al - ways feeds. Oh,'

Chorus

why, tell me why, does you stand in de rain, Oh,

why does you suf - fer from sick - ness and pain, For all ob

you is God's chill-un, and he's goin' to give you what you needs.

Gimmie Song

I know I'se one ob God's chillun,
An' he's goin' to gimmie what I needs—
I know I'se one ob de select elect—
One ob de chillun God always feeds.

Chorus:
Oh, why do you stand in de snow and de rain,
Oh, why do you suffer from sickness and pain.
'Cause all ob you belongs to God,
An' he's goin' to gib you what you need.

Notice how, in the chorus, the singer deliberately declared the therapeutic value of belonging to God. Although he ran out of really big ideas after the first verse and chorus, the other two verses are interesting in the pictures they present.

Oh, Moses hit dat desert rock—
De Good Book up an' tells us so,
While all de brethren stood hard by,
Wonderin' if de water would really flow.
(*Chorus*).

Parson says I'll baptize you,
So's all your sins'll pass away.
He ducked me down mid shouts and prayers—
'Fore God, dat wuz a happy day.
(*Chorus*).

Among the boys of William's outfit, a song had sprung into existence which illustrated the effect of army discipline on the slow, easy-going Southern negro. Fighting a war demands movement, speed, and action—but most of all it demands something few of the Southern negroes of William's type understood—instantaneous action.

SCRATCH

Scratch your lousy...... back, scratch your lousy

back. Pick up your gun and swing your pack, 'Cause

Kais-er William's on your track. Scratch your lou - sy back.

The line "scratch your lousy back" had no reference to brushing off a stray louse or two. What it really means is, "pull yourself together," "snap into it," "both feet on the deck and do it NOW."

Scratch Your Lousy Back

Scratch your lousy back, scratch your lousy back,
Pick up your gun and swing your pack,
'Cause Kaiser William's on your track,
Scratch your lousy back.

Scratch your lousy back, scratch your lousy back,
Keep your head down in dis trench,
Or you're never goin' to see dat little high brown wench,
Scratch your lousy back.

Scratch your lousy back, scratch your lousy back,
Whenever you hear the rattlin' of bully beef tins,
You better grab for your gas mask and be sorry for your sins,
Scratch your lousy back.

As I recovered the use of my legs, I took to exploring that hospital, and, being rather a privileged character, there were few crannies or cubby-holes I didn't get into sooner or later.

One morning a colored lad who had been very badly gassed attracted my attention by waving a scrap of newspaper at me. In a very weak voice he told me that he knew a song I should surely add to my collection—it was the song about hanging various members of the Imperial German family on a sour-apple tree. This was immensely amusing to both of us. I laughed aloud, while he went through the motions of laughing without uttering more than a raspy gurgle. Our conversation was interrupted by a nurse and some attendants who came to take him away for some treatment or other. As I left he asked me if I would get him a newspaper. I explained that *The Herald, The Tribune,* or *The Mail* were rarely found in St. Denis, but that I would try.

When I came back next afternoon—a screen of sheets—hospital fashion—shielded him from view—he was "going west"—I had come too late—his song was "going west" with him.

At the window near by I tore the single-folded French newspaper into little squares—and let them flutter slowly from my trembling hands.

Across the garden just below, where the gloom of early evening was already gathering, one might hear the noise of clattering dishes, the evening meal in preparation. But somehow in my ears I seemed to hear soft voices gently singing—

> Don't close dose gates,
> 'Cause I'm sure comin' in.
> Don't close dose gates,
> 'Cause I'm sure comin' in.

* * *

WHO SAID GAS?

CHAPTER IV

(November 11th, 1918.—Walked in on the boys while they were at mess. Have to use two canes to make any forward speed, but that's better than being strapped to a board in the hospital. At nine o'clock the radio operators intercepted messages from the long-wave station in Germany in reference to a possible armistice. Our major received confirmation of armistice rumor later from 45 Avenue Montaigne. At eleven o'clock all the whistles and anti-aircraft batteries in Paris cut loose. We knew that the war was over for the present. We didn't know whether to be glad or not. The first thing we talked about was our lost thirty-three and one-third per cent—the good lads who had been bumped off. All flying was called off after mess. About three in the afternoon the Gas-House Gang went to town (Paris) to help celebrate. They wouldn't let me go—said I'd get lost in the mob. Johnnie was appointed to stay home and keep me company.)

(November 12th, 1918.—The boys took me to town to-night. Big John Bailey took care of me when the crowds got too thick. I never experienced such a night in my life—the boys said that the second night was better than the first.)

SO—the Armistice was signed—the Germans coming out second-best, after nearly every one thought they had the war won two or three times. The next logical thing was the Peace Treaty and the payment of war indemnities —a Peace Treaty that would be another "scrap of paper" and war indemnities that would make the paying nations more bitter against the victors than they were before the war began. Then the victors had to pay their debts to one another, and finally, both victor and vanquished found it

88

necessary to provide in some measure for the wounded, the disabled, and the fatherless. In short, the backwash had to be raked away. Departments were established where bureaucrats dispensed the divers rewards nations usually confer upon their disabled defenders. Societies for the outlawing of war sprung up, and the antimilitaristic membership, as usual, hindered the progress of peace among nations. War is a form of blow-off. As far back as we are able to make any form of reasonable investigations, we find that men drank intoxicating drinks or narcoticized certain brain centres by the use of any means they had handy—hunted wild animals—fought duels—laughed, played, danced, used profanity—went to sexual excesses, etc., as a form of relaxation. Then when these forms of relaxation were no longer sufficient, they went to war. And the highly evolved modern man is not so far different from his prehistoric brethren, except that he goes through the silly procedure of signing a treaty, and then has to break it. The Hindu philosophers knew that war was a futile procedure thousands of years ago.

> Better live on beggar's bread
>   With those we love alive,
> Than taste their blood in rich feasts spread,
>   And guiltily survive.
> Ah, were it worse who knows to be
>   Victor or vanquished here,
> When those confront us angrily,
>   Whose death leaves living drear.
>   (*Song Celestial—Bhagavad Gita.*)

Some smart person is either going to make the majority of this planet's population think seriously about peace or find a substitute for war, and in the meanwhile we'll most

probably fight, or get licked—and fighting in these days of
modern warfare is an ordeal, from which one recovers slowly.

* * *

As soon as we were sure the Armistice was signed, some
of our boys put in for immediate return to the States. We
who stayed in France have since discovered the folly of going
home too soon. Those days early in 1919 were lean days—
business was bad—jobs were scarce—and living was high.
The ones who voluntarily stayed in France after the signing of the armistice and finished up the job were smart and
didn't know it—at least, they didn't know it at the time.

In November and December, 1918, we flew many ships
to the new front (the Rhine) to supply the squadrons there.
We also picked up strays—ships we had been forced to land
at some out-of-the-way field—ships that after a few hours
of repairing were ready to go again.

About the 20th of November, after demonstrating in a
short flight that I hadn't lost my nerve, orders were given
me to pick up one of these forced landings at the little
French field near Provins, and fly it to Vinets. Another
pilot on our field was given orders at the same time to pick
up a similar ship at Malmaison. We started out together,
intending to motor by way of Paris, first to Malmaison and
then to Provins. My partner conceived the idea of taking a
girl friend of his along, and having me fly her to Vinets (my
ship being a two-place Salmson). I have never known
that girl's full name—to me she was Irene, a Red Cross girl
from Chicago, very pretty, very modest, and very anxious
to fly. We called for her at a hotel in the neighborhood of
the Place Concorde, my friend making a play of not knowing exactly where she lived. He seemed to think I should

be impressed with the idea that she and he were only very casually acquainted, although it was an unimportant detail. After the first half-hour of the trip I knew this was not the case.

We lunched at Brie Comte Robert. The pièce de résistance was a pheasant. What a dinner! The delicious fall air had made us ravenously hungry. We were at table easily two hours. From Brie Comte Robert we went to Malmaison, where my partner left us to fly his one-place Spad. At the Provins field I discovered that my Salmson was in bad condition. First, the motor wouldn't turn up the required number of revolutions (usually called "revs"), then the landing and flying wires were saggy. The ship had a sad-looking air about it. Irene began to lose interest in her proposed flight. I told my chauffeur to stand by in case she didn't decide to fly, as it would have been unfortunate to leave her flat at that French field with no easy way of getting back to the city. After making numerous motor tests, Irene and I held a consultation. I thought the motor would turn over a little more in the air. But girls had been bad luck to pilots before. I had visions of a smashed Salmson with two people crawling out of it. No! I'd fly alone.

The field was surrounded by trees on three sides and by a line of telephone-wires on the fourth. The trees looked like a softer thing to fall on if the motor went absolutely dead. So, after waving Irene good-by, I taxied out and took off in the direction of the lowest trees. Instead of reving up higher as the trees came closer, the motor fell off a bit, but it was too late to stop. I opened the throttle as wide as it would go, held my wheels on the ground until the last possible moment, swallowed, turned my head to one side, and pulled back on the controls with everything I had. The

undercarriage skimmed the tops of the trees by such a narrow margin that the wind from the propeller blew a gust
of reddish brown leaves behind as I passed over. With the
extra 110 pounds weight and the bad-luck idea the female
passenger would have provided in the back seat, I would
never have been able to get that ship over those trees. As
it was, for the next half-hour I flew just over the top of
French kitchen-gardens and backyards, skimming trees and
church-spires by the narrowest of margins. I tried all the
possible manipulations of the air and gasoline levers, but
the motor missed and coughed as if it were just about to
drop me in the middle of some Frenchman's butter-bean
patch. When I did finally land at the Vinets field, it was
raining. One of the pilots permanently attached to the field
asked me what the orders were on my ship.

"According to the orders, it's supposed to go to Collombey les Belles from here, but if I were you, I'd just back it
out yonder in one of those far hangars and let it rot. It
won't take long."

I never saw our Red Cross friend after that. She must
have arrived back in Paris safely, in spite of her disappoint-
ment at not making a flight. The pilot who picked up the
Spad told me later that he took her along on the supposi-
tion that his ship would not fly at all—then he and the girl
should have had the motor-car and the chauffeur at their
disposal to tour about France a bit. He admitted, however,
that the girl was not in on his plan. She was interested in
flying, not touring.

I should never have recounted this pointless tale if I hadn't
encountered a truck-load of singing colored lads at Troyes on
the way back to Orly. Among their equipment I noticed
musical instruments. The officer in charge of them (a very

dapper looking second lieutenant) told me that they had just played a performance at a near-by camp. We discussed the negro as a singing soldier. The colored officer was surprised that any one had gone to the trouble to record the random singing of the black boys. After I had sung him some of the tunes in my collection, however, he agreed that they were worth writing off. Among his boys there were several very talented singers—one of them a blues singer, who did the regulation St. Louis blues, etc., in a marvellously characteristic manner. But the regulation blues can be bought in every music-store in the land.

I didn't begin to take notice until the blues expert sang one of his own concoctions—a version of the "moving" blues. Instead of having the "moving-man sadness," he had the "soldier-man sadness." His third, fourth, and fifth verses were out of the picture. They had no connection with the war or the blueness of soldiering, but they were so naïve that I could not refrain from including them in the text of the song.

These are the verses of "The Soldier Man Blues." He began with the chorus, as usual.

This is the principal motif of the "Soldier Man Blues."

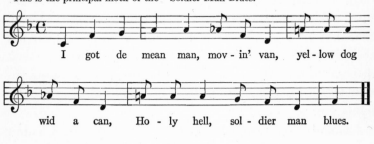

I got de mean man, mov - in' van, yel - low dog
wid a can, Ho - ly hell, sol - dier man blues.

Chorus:

I got the soldier man sadness, the soldier man blues,
I want to do what I want and I want to do it when I choose.

peat !

I got de mean man, moving van, yellow dog wid a can—
Holy hell, soldier man blues.

(1)

I'd rather be a pimpin' fur one-eyed Kate, and do a first-
class job at a cut-price rate,
Than tote a gun in this man's war, er drive a noisy motorcycle side car.
(*Chorus.*)

(2)

For Lizzie's a gal widout much style, but you should see
those papas caper when she puts out her smile,
While one-eyed Kate is full o' speed and she bends in the
middle like a broken reed.
(*Chorus.*)

(3)

Now I know colored folks is always tryin' to find a way to
git to heaven by slippin' 'round behind,
But Peter's always standin' wid a mallet in 'is hand, only
lettin' of de chosen enter in de promised land.
(*Chorus.*)

Steam train standin' on de railroad track—couldn't go forward so he had to go back,
Steam train man wuz a singin' sad, cause 'is engine acted up
so bad.
(*Chorus.*)

'Possum a hangin' on a hickory limb—moon wuz a shinin'
down on him,
'Possum simply ain't no use 'less he's a floatin' in a puddle
o' pot liquor juice.
———————————— (*Chorus.*)

Repeat
chorus.

One of my wild-goose chases in the latter part of November, 1918, took me down in the direction of Bordeaux. On
the return trip I received an invitation to a very novel
hunting expedition—a boar hunt, where the hunters rode

through the underbrush on U. S. Army tractors, armed with army rifles. The boar hunt was a failure—partly due to intoxicated drivers (who ditched one of the tractors) and partly due to the noise made by the exhaust of the engines. But the boar hunt brought me in contact with a colored boy (my host's orderly) who provided my diary with some of its choicest notes. This is a specimen conversation:

"Duz de lootenant s'pose dis here war will be over in 'bout two weeks? I mean, will we be shuttin' up shop and goin' home?"

"Oh, damit to hell, Elmer, I've told you a hundred times —NO!"

"But, lootenant, I wants to git back in time to plant my sweet potato crop."

"Now listen, Elmer, once and for all, the war is over— has been since the 11th of this month,—but that doesn't mean that you're goin' back to Mississippi, or wherever you live, in two weeks. What are you goin' to do about all that barbed wire, open trenches, unexploded shells, dud bombs? No, Elmer, you'll have to help 'em clean up that front."

"But, lootenant, I wants to git home so's I can plant my sweet potato crop. An' I always lays out my simlin hills* real early-like, so's they mellow up 'fore I puts in de seeds. 'Course I wouldn't mind to putter 'round wid wire an' trenches, but dud bombs, nossar! No dud bombs fur Elmer. I'm afeared I mought tickle de fusin' contraption. No vine- gar poultice 'd ever cure Elmer from dud bomb explo- sions."

He was shining a pair of boots and a Sam Browne belt.

"'Course, I'm broke most o' de time, 'cause o' my allot- ment. See, I got a wife. We wuzn't married in a church-

* Simlin—the negro word for "Simnel"—a type of squash.

house—we wuz married by de ring ceremony. I gives her a ring, then we's married. When she wants to git unmarried, she hands de ring back. When dey wuz draftin' at de Court-House, I tole 'em I wuz married—thought I mought git free 'cause of my wife. They asked me, did I ever give her any money? I says nossar—she gives me money, though. So I went to war. Now if it wuzn't fur you all hepin' me out, I'd be broke always. Yessar, my wife come to the train-shed to see me go away. She wuz wearin' her new bee-gum hat—um-hum. I sho' wants to go back."

It took Elmer all morning to make four beds and straighten up the room they were in, and all afternoon to do the washing and shine the leather for the four officers he was assigned to as orderly. The officers saw that Elmer was well taken care of—and Elmer would not have traded his job for any assignment in the United States Army.

La Courneau was a so-called recuperation and rest camp. Whenever there was no other place to send a contingent of men, they were sent off to La Courneau. It had originally been used by the French. A rumor was abroad that a considerable number of Russians had been finished off at La Courneau. They had mutinied. It was a mysterious kind of place—a place where anything might happen. There were many American officers in La Courneau—awaiting transportation to America or a return to their outfits. La Courneau bored them terribly. They were constantly A. W. O. L.

The signing of the armistice was a signal for going loose. Bordeaux, 50 kilometres away, was not an uncheerful place the night of the 11th of November, but Paris went mad—and La Courneau went to Paris. During the week following the signing of the armistice, M. P.'s brought back whole detachments of officers and men to La Courneau. That's why the jail-house at La Courneau was so full. And it was a mean jail-house. Elmer warned every one away from it.

"Don't go in it, lootenant, even if you duz have to defend dose hoboes in de courts martial. Talk to 'em through a hole in de fence—dey'll abbreviate yo' life if you go in—dat's a mean jail-house."

One of the keepers had a pile of brickbats handy. If an inmate stuck his head over the top of the palisade, a brickbat would come sailing over at him. This was an unfortunate procedure; the inmates kept the brickbats that fell in the enclosure, and it is said they used them in several emergencies to the disadvantage of the guards and keepers. It was a mean jail-house. There were men in there for every crime covered by the "Manual of Courts Martial."

"Duz de lootenant feel porely?"

"Yes, Elmer, I've had a sore throat ever since that dumb damn boar hunt."

"I 'lowed dat boar hunt wun't git nobody much. De tractor makes such of a noise—boar simply hauls his freight. I 'lowed somebody 'ud come out o' dat boar hunt second best. Has de lootenant tried wrappin' up de throat wid a sock? I never has no miseries in my throat, 'cause I has me a "assifidity" bag, an' cucumber-seeds fur kernels."

"Cucumber-seeds? Why, Elmer, what are you trying to tell me?"

"Yessar, cucumber-seeds carried in de left hip-pocket is sho' cure for kernels in de jaw and sore throat."

Elmer did carry both cucumber-seeds and an asafetida-bag. The bag had been hanging around his neck so long that it had darkened down to the color of his skin. His clothing smelled terribly of the fetid drug. All sickness to Elmer was a device of the devil. The cucumber-seeds and

the asafetida-bag were fairly good charms, but now and
again the "voodoo" could not be overcome—Elmer would
be taken down with a misery. He'd sing about it.

> Oh, I got a misery in my innards—
> Work ob de devil—
> Ole man devil—
> Oh, I got a misery in my innards—
> God's goin' to chase it away.

But the miseries, the sweet potato crop in Mississippi, the
wife in the beegum-hat (who was slightly outside the pale
in not having the background of a church-house wedding),
the wire, the trenches, and the dud bombs, were of little or
no importance, when compared to the agonizing thought of
sea travel.

On the way to France, Elmer had suffered from a new
kind of blues—the deep-sea variety. They had been set to
music. And what blues! The tale of his trip to Hoboken
and later to Bordeaux was an epic. He admitted that he
did not understand what the draft was all about at the time
of enlistment, nor did many of his fellows. They were sent
north shortly after being outfitted—sent to Hoboken where
they worked on the docks. Elmer said he rather thought
that he'd been caught in some practical joke or other, when
one day what seemed to be the warehouse, floated away.
The "Deep-Sea Blues" tells this phase of the tale very ac-
curately:

> Everybody in Hoboken town—everybody an' me,
> Hopped upon a warehouse that was swinging around
> An' went to sea.
> Oh, all day long I'se a lookin' for trees,
> Lookin' for sand, lookin' for land,

> 'Cause I've got dose awful weepin', sleepin',
> Got dose awful sailin', wailin',
> Got dose awful deep-sea blues.

His lyrics were not consistent—they varied with the particular kind of misery he had come down with, but the blues were always of the deep sea, and the deep sea was something he intended to avoid in his future life,

> "Ef God prospers me and gives me life, AMEN."

The unfortunate death and burial of some colored soldiers at sea had made a profound impression on him. This fact had crept into the Blues.

> Soldiers down below layin' cold and dead—
> Everybody 'cept me—
> Drop 'em over side loaded down wid lead—
> While we'se at sea.
> Oh, all day long, etc.

He had one verse about "de devil ridin' 'bout in a submarine," and one involving President Wilson, but they were not recorded. The importance of the negro in the winning of the war made up the other verse:

> All dese colored soldiers comin' over to France,
> All dese soldiers and me,
> Goin' to help de whites make de Kaiser dance,
> All dese soldiers an' me.
> Oh, all day long, etc.

This last verse was no doubt invented after the arrival of Elmer's outfit in France,—after they had had an opportunity really to find out what the war was about and to become conversant about such persons as the Kaiser.

"An' I 'spose dat de lootenant knows 'bout de battle-

DEEP–SEA BLUES

Arranged by J. J. N.

Ev - ery - bod - y in Ho - - bo - ken town,

ev - ery-bod -y and me Hopped up - on a warehouse dat was

swing-in' a - round   and went to sea.
(we went to sea)

All day long I'm a look-in' for trees, Look-in' for land, I'm a

look - in' for sand, 'Cause I got dose sleep - in', weep - in',

Got dose sail-in', wail- in', Oh, I got dose aw-ful deep-sea blues.

royal in the Officers' Mess to-night? Yessar, but Elmer don't git into no battle-royals. I didn't draft myself into no army fur to git slugged in a free-fur-all. An' I s'pose de lootenant done heared 'bout de new bunch o' bozos in de

'CAUSE I GOT DOSE AWFUL DEEP-SEA BLUES

jail-house. One o' them is in fur a new kind o' charge—tryin' to sell a locomotive to a Frenchman—it wuz a USA locomotive."

"And just let me have that grayish-looking book, the tall one—thanks, Elmer."

"Oh, yessar, I done hear tell o' dat book. It tells 'bout how you can git to Leavensworth. An' duz de lootenant know ef dandelion greens grows in France? I craves a mess o' dandelion, particular ef dey ain't got no cucker burs in 'em. An' lootenant, would it be askin' too much . . .?"

(Diary note. Romorantin. Liberty assembling and testing-field, December 12, 1918.)

The Chicken Butcher (who gained his name from a pre-war vocation) had used his razor with too lavish a hand, and thereupon had been caused to do time in Black Jack's Jail-House at Jevres. (General John J. Pershing was known to some of the colored boys as "Black Jack.") Life in Black Jack's Jail-House had chastened the Chicken Butcher—chastened him more than one would expect. He had even (without knowing it) taken to practising a very efficient modern spiritual belief. He was curing his waywardness by continually affirming his desire to be good. The Chicken Butcher possessed the childish simplicity and naïveté so seldom found in the present cycle of the black man's development. He had set his affirmation of righteousness to music —or perhaps it had set itself to music—if music it may be called. The tune covered what is known to musicians as a fifth.

CHICKEN BUTCHER

Oh, jail-house key, don't you ev-er lock me in.   Oh,

jail-house key, won't nev-er be bad no more.   Oh,(etc.)

Oh, jail-house key,
Don't you ever lock me in.
Oh, jail-house key—
Won't never be bad no more.

Oh, chickenfoot grass,
You points three ways to heaven.
Oh, chickenfoot grass,
Won't never be bad no more.

Oh, turkey-wing brush,
You brushes up dem ashes,
Oh, turkey-wing brush,
Won't never be bad no more.

Oh, dark ob de moon—
Don't you ever blight my life. . . .
Oh, dark ob de moon—
Won't never be bad no more.

Oh, garbage can—
You smells to high heaven. . . .
Oh, garbage can—
Won't never be bad no more.

Oh, razor hone—
You sharpens up mv slasher. . . .
Oh, razor hone—
Won't never be bad no more.

Oh, chitlin supper—
Oh, chitlin supper wid beer. . . .
Oh, chitlin supper—
Won't never be bad no more.

Oh, lightnin' bug—
Don't you burn your pants—
Oh, lightnin' bug—
Won't never be bad no more.

Oh, jail-house blues—
How blue you can be. . . .
Oh, jail-house blues—
Won't never be bad no more.

On one of my last few flights to Collombey les Belles, I
was forced to land at a French field about two kilometres
from St. Dizier. The ground was covered with snow on
which a thin skim of ice had frozen. I misjudged my forward speed in landing and ran into a hangar. The front
flaps were closed. I took off one wing and damaged the propeller. It took the repair-department from Collombey les
Belles four days to get my ship back in the air again. During those four days I had many telephone conversations with
the operations officer back at Orly. It was while waiting one
day for a long distance connection with Orly that a Signal
Corps sergeant presented Dog Star, and had him sing his
"Jackass Song" for me.

"I don't see why you-all wants to hear me sing—particular, when it's 'bout a mule. Course, ef de sergeant says I
duz, I duz. Original-like, dis jackass belonged to a machine-
gun outfit. He got hit but wasn't lucky enough to die.
Frien' o' mine, a Jug Band player, made up part o' dis song,
an' I made up part. No jackass ever set on no grenade.
Now, a Springfield totin' soldier might be dumb enough to
do such of a thing, but a jackass knows what's good fur 'im
—jus' like a colored man an' a owl. Dey wuz usin' dis mule
around a dump o' dis here German truck. One day mos'
near a whole box o' potato-mashers went off. Dat Jug Band
player ain't never been no use since. Now, before some fool
screwed a handle into one o' dose grenades, dat mule wuz
a whole hoss, wagon, and team, but when dat box o' mashers
turned loose, it was Kingdom Come."

Jackass what wuz named ole Henry,
Jackass workin' for a soldier man.
Jackass what wuz named old Henry,
Don't you go near dat powder can.

Jackass what wuz named ole Henry,
Jackass what wuz always late.
Jackass what wuz named ole Henry,
Jackass you bes' haul yo' freight.

Jackass what wuz named ole Henry,
Jackass see de mess you made—
Jackass what wuz named ole Henry,
Sot down on a hand grenade.

Jackass when dis war is over,
Jackass don't you never mind.
You'll be fertilizin' clover,
When dis treaty's done been signed.
    Goo'-by, Jackass.

His chant-like tune was limited to the span of only six notes. The singer (known as "Dog Star" from having been born during dog days) was from southern Louisiana, where the influence of Roman Catholic Church music is so generally found in the songs of the negroes.

Dog Star was detailed to barracks' police, in place of a colored boy, who, several days previous, had been discovered standing behind a stove in a petrified state of drunkenness, from overconsumption of lemon extract. But barracks' policing did not become Dog Star—he was essentially an out-of-doors man—a soldier around whom a legend had been constructed. Among the members of his outfit he had become known as a "hard-fightin' sonovabitch." It was evident that he had never quite recovered from the hand-to-hand encounter that had gained him a decoration and reputation. When the regular barracks' orderly recovered from the lemon-extract jag, Dog Star would go back to his mule-driving detail.

He drove a span of very much scarred-up animals. He had named one of them "Fool" and the other "Dummy." His conversations with these erstwhile machine-gun jack-asses were poetic.

"Why, Dummy, what's de matter wif you? Ain't you done heared me tell you to jump up? An' you, Fool, tighten up dose traces. I'll have to bounce a wagon-tongue off yo' hollow head. Come on, Dummy, do yo' stuff. Jump up in here, Fool."

The naming of these animals Fool and Dummy was thought to be in some way prophetic. His story was passed on by a "fed-up" machine-gunner, wearing a silver bar and an M. P. brassard. It seems that although Dog Star was an infantryman himself, he had very little respect for soldiers who "toted" Springfields, or artillerymen (he called them "seventy-fivers"), or rifle-grenadiers. In his estimation, automatic-riflemen, bandolier-carriers, and clip-toters were the real winners of the war. He had even been doubtful of clip-carriers. Through a judgment too quickly formed, he had condemned members of his own team.

During the later days of the war, Dog Star's outfit was operating in a hilly stretch of country between the Moselle and the Sielle Rivers. Dog Star had been armed with a French chaut-chaut automatic. To him the automatic weapon was a "sho-shot" rifle. Although it was a crude, almost unlovely weapon, Dog Star never tired of shining, oiling, and caressing his sho-shot.

The Boche had a method of regaining lost territory by a

process known as infiltration. Through the failure of an outfit near by to maintain proper liaison, Dog Star's platoon
found itself exposed on the right. Here an infiltration of
German infantry made the unprotected right flank bristle

with trouble. Through the early fall twilight Dog Star and
his team made their way. Their objective was the remains
of a German trench system on the brow of a little hill some
hundred metres off. They passed the battered remains of a
tank. It lay like some monstrous prehistoric turtle, where,

to the delight of the enemy, it had slipped into a well-laid tank-trap. The French artillerymen, who knew to a metre the location of the trap, had pounded the once powerful mechanism into an inert mass of smoking junk.

Dog Star's last stand was on the rim of a small-sized shell-hole. Here he expended his ammunition against everything that moved. A shell fell near by. Dog Star looked for the other members of his team. He had used his last clip. The

"IT HAD SLIPPED INTO A WELL-LAID TANK-TRAP"

other members of his outfit had disappeared,—those bandolier-carriers were yellow, goddam 'em! What could a soldier do with a funny French "sho-shot" and no clips! And then he suddenly found himself confronted by men in greenish gray uniforms—greenish gray uniforms and tub-shaped hats. He still held the useless chaut-chaut in his hands. It weighed less than twenty pounds, but backed up with his fiendish strength it was a veritable battering-ram. The ground was covered with mausers and unexploded grenades, but the

blood of forgotten races of black savages surged in his veins.
He was not a mathematician, a linguist, an intellectual dil-
letante. He had reverted back to the tribesmen in the upper
Nile Valley. He no longer understood the mechanisms of
modern warfare, but his sense of aim was perfect—his desire
to live, supreme. His thought of fear vanished—he fought
as a savage. The clipless chaut-chaut gun swung in a wide
circle, squashing tub-shaped hats down upon greenish gray

DOG STAR AND HIS "SHO-SHOT"

shoulders. But somehow one man couldn't hold out long
against seven. The butt of a Mauser hit Dog Star in the
back of the head. He went down. And it was very suddenly
night.

The remains of the platoon and some strays from a
machine-gun outfit arrived. They had witnessed the last

few moments of Dog Star's performance. It was through them that he gained his reputation—a hard-fightin' sonova-bitch. A few tense periods of excitement followed their ar-rival. Several hysterical bursts of machine-gun fire. Fuses were pulled on a few potato-mashers—and silence!

It rained later on in the night, and to Dog Star's great dis-comfort, he found that he could not move the upper part of his body—something had happened to his neck. But the rain was very cooling. He tried to roll over on his back so that he might catch some drops in his mouth. In the morn-ing he was picked up by some stretcher-bearers. As the bearers passed a near-by shell-hole, they paused to look at two figures who seemed to be asleep. They were the other members of Dog Star's team. They were sitting up quite straight—and very dead! The third member was a few paces away—lying face down. After all, those clip-toters were not yellow. The shell that fell just before Dog Star ran out of ammunition had caught all three of them.

"An' what do you spose dose Hineys tried to do? Kill a nigger by hittin' 'im on de head. Now, if dey'd a cracked me on de shins, it 'ud been de same as dat mule and de grenades—kingdom come!"

* * *

As 1918 turned to 1919, flying days were very scarce. . . . To celebrate Christmas we had a grand party. . . . Many guests came from far and near, knowing that a party at the Orly flying-field had never been known to miss fire. . . . After the first of the year some of our boys had orders to go home, that is to say they had orders to go as far as Bor-deaux (where they stayed a good long while). . . . Others went on extended leaves. . . . Those who remained at camp

Jack-ass what was named Ole Hen-ry, Jack-ass
work-in' for a sol-dier man; Jack-ass what was
named Ole Hen-ry, Don't you sit on dat pow-der can.

took advantage of non-flying days to make the trip to Paris.
. . . Certain groups could have been seen night after night
at the Opera Comique, The Apollo, the Folies Bergère,
etc. . . .

During the latter part of January (1919) one of our boys
was reported a casualty. . . . He had been known as a wild
flier, but a lucky one. . . . The gas-house mourned him.
. . . The heartbreaking procedure of rolling up his belong-
ings had just been assigned to one of his most intimate
friends, when in he walked. . . . That was a signal for a
celebration. . . . An orderly was dispatched to Choisy le
Roi for a supply of liquor. . . . The boys were all called in
. . . the party began. . . .

* * *

A mixture of rum, champagne, brown sugar, and spices,
had been heated and sipped—steaming in half-pint tin cups.
Then the mixture was mixed again. And again! And again!
And again! Outside it rained. But with a certain amount
of poking, the fire of French brickets had dispelled the pen-
etrating cold. Inside it was so cosey! A speech was in
progress—"Our Duty to Our Women Folk Back Home."
The phrases were not all coherent, nor the basic reasonings
sound, but the boys "yehed" the speaker at every pause.

"Baldy" had been talking about life. Life was a serious
affair to-night. "Might go out to fly to-morrow and bump
off"—bump off and be no more seen. "Pour me a li'l, too.
Thanks, Swede, ole boy."

The one who had been in the French Ambulance Service
before he had transferred to the air always sang about this
time. To-night he reverted to the "We Wish the Same to
You" song.

WE WISH THE SAME TO YOU

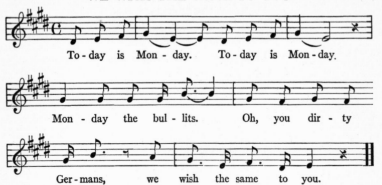

To - day is Mon - day.   To - day is Mon - day.

Mon - day the bul - lits.   Oh, you dir - ty

Ger - mans,   we   wish   the same   to   you.

"WE WISH THE SAME TO YOU" SONG

To-day is Monday—
To-day is Monday—
Monday the bullets—
Oh, you dirty Germans,
We wish the same to you.

To-day is Tuesday—
To-day is Tuesday—
Monday the bullets—
Tuesday the bayonets—
Oh, you dirty Germans—
We wish the same to you.

To-day is Wednesday—
To-day is Wednesday—
Monday the bullets—
Tuesday the bayonets—
Wednesday the shrapnel—
Oh, you dirty Germans—
We wish the same to you.

To-day is Thursday—
To-day is Thursday—
Monday the bullets—
Tuesday the bayonets—
Wednesday the shrapnel—
Thursday the mustard gas—
Oh, you dirty Germans—
We wish the same to you.

To-day is Friday—
To-day is Friday—
Monday the bullets—
Tuesday the bayonets—
Wednesday the shrapnel—
Thursday the mustard gas—
Friday the dressing station—
Oh, you dirty Germans—
We wish the same to you.

To-day is Saturday—
To-day is Saturday—
Monday the bullets—
Tuesday the bayonets—
Wednesday the shrapnel—
Thursday the mustard gas—
Friday the ambulance—
Saturday the hospital—
Oh, you dirty Germans—
We wish the same to you.

To-day is Sunday—
To-day is Sunday—
Monday the bullets—
Tuesday the bayonets—
Wednesday the shrapnel—
Thursday the mustard gas—
Friday the ambulance—

> Saturday the hospital—
> Sunday the graveyard—
> Oh, you dirty Germans—
> We wish the same to you.

"Now, listen, Perry, that was well done. But why in hell do you always have to drag in graveyards? You're as bad as 'Tombstone Smith' and 'is bloody dog-goned monument-mill."

"Yeah! I'm a lone wolf. It's my night out and I'll have my howl. Yeah. Whoopee!"

> Here's to good ole rum—
> Drink 'er down—drink 'er down—
> Here's to good ole rum,
> Drink 'er down—drink 'er down.
> Here's to good ole rum,
> That makes me feel so bum,
> Here's to good ole rum,
> Drink 'er down—drink 'er down.

The drinking-match had reached a point of frenzy. It was all because of the return of one who had been reported, "Down, out of control"! Indeed, a pilot had stepped from the casualty list, with a slight limp, a black eye (that was yellowing into recovery), an excellent aviation-clock (salvaged from the wrecked ship) and a whale of a good story.

> Here's to good ole liquor—
> Drink 'er down—drink 'er down—
> Here's to good ole liquor—
> Drink 'er down—drink 'er down.

"Yeah, stop it! Yu simply can't sing that song an' use the word 'liquor.' Shimpossible. Won't rhyme with nothin'. I've tried it many's a time."

There was a discreet knock on the barracks' door.

"Come in, if you can git in."

It was the colonel's orderly—and a very sleepy-eyed orderly at that.

"Colonel's respects to the lieutenants."

The pilot who had been wearing the Polish drinking-hat most of the evening assumed charge of the situation.

"No, wait, boy. Did the colonel say 'respects,' or did he say 'compliments'? We mush 'ave all the faks."

"Sorry, sir, don't remember, sir. But bein's it's past two o'clock, the colonel would like to ask the lieutenants to pipe down a little."

"Now, boy, listen. I know we've been loud. We've been boisterous. Yea, verily, I say we've even been hilarious. But how do you suppose we can win the war if the enlisted personnel can't remember what their commandin' officer says to 'em?"

"Sorry, sir; I'll mention what the lieutenant just said, to the colonel."

> Oh, the colonel, he's a jolly ole soul,
> Do we love 'im—
> I'll say we do.
> Oh, the colonel, he's a jolly ole soul——

"Say, you inebriate bums, can't you, for the love of God, batten down a little? I've got to test a lot of ships to-morrow. An' one of 'em is a monoplane. I need some sleep."

"Now listen, buddy. Don't worry about sleep. After you fly that old monoplane, you may not need no sleep—ever think o' that?"

Three boys sat in front of the fire. The others staggered into bed. One lad found that the leaking roof had transformed his bedding-roll into a miniature lake—but Loco's

bed was dry. Loco'd been knocked off a few days past—
they hadn't rolled his stuff up yet. Some one opened the
stove-door. A square beam of rose-colored light fell on the
wall. Baldy broke a long silence——

"An' boys, I've come to a conclusion. Life is like a lake.
'Round the side o' the lake grows short grass and bushes.
In the middle o' the lake sits sex—floatin' on a beautiful
barge. An' we're all crawlin' round in the short grass and
bushes, tryin' to git out there to 'er."

No answer. The pilot who had stepped out of the pages
of the casualty lists with a limp and a black eye, thought a
lot. But no one seemed to have an answer to Baldy's conclusion about life.

* * *

CHAPTER V

IN front of the Sanger Hall fireplace, on the night of the 19th of February, 1919, our major inadvertently gave out the news about closing Orly. We had flown many ships to and from Orly—Spads, SE5's, the old wiggly-winged Sops, Salmsons, Moraines, FE2B's, Caudrons, Libertys, Breguets, Voisins, Camels, etc. . . . Many ships had been flown into Orly, equipped with guns, tested and flown away to the front. . . . But now the hangars were nearly empty —a few ships remained. . . . These we would fly to Romorantin, put them on the million-dollar bonfire, and the job would be over. . . .

We were unwilling to believe that our flying-days were over. . . . That the festive rum-cooking matches over the stove in our barracks (the Gas-House) would soon be history. . . . But the hangars were nearly empty—the date for clearing out was set—we were to "ring down" on March the 1st. . . . After that, no one knew just what. . . .

The major was all for closing camp with a bang. . . . He remembered the 1918 Christmas party. . . . We'd have another—Washington's Birthday. . . . We'd invite all the Red Cross and Y. M. C. A. girls we knew. . . . We'd decorate the officers' mess. . . . We'd open bottles that pop and fizz. . . . We'd eclipse all other A. E. F. parties so far reported. . . . The major said that the outside edge of the sky was the limit. . . .

German helmets, empty shell-cases, wicker projectile-baskets, etc., were to be used in the decorative scheme. . . . I

119

was supplied the assistance of another member of the Gas-House, four enlisted men, a camion, an extra bedon of gasoline, and orders to return with the needed German paraphernalia. . . . (The major referred to it as a truck-load of Heinie junk to be used as "atmosphere." . . .)

Before noon the next day we, the junk-collectors, passed through the battered town of Soissons, headed for the battlefields on both sides of the Soissons-Laon road, where Hosky, my Gas-House assistant, the second-in-command of our two-day expedition, had operated in the early days of the war as an ambulance-man with the French Field Service. . . . The enlisted men in our detail were revelling in a good time. . . . We had given them absolute orders not to touch anything having the slightest suspicious appearance—unexploded shells, hand-grenades, explosives, etc. . . .

They worked diligently for the first three or four hours, sorting out the best camouflaged helmets, the best-looking shell-baskets, etc., but as evening came on, the desire to shoot off a few firecrackers became stronger and stronger. . . .

Hosky and I were examining a German field-telephone exchange, just under the brow of that first hill on the right side of the Soissons-Laon road, wondering what the major would say if we brought it back to camp, when, all of a sudden, we heard an explosion, followed by a mighty and continuous roar. . . . Hosky involuntarily stepped back into the subterranean trench system a moment. . . . Then together we hurried out to see just what had happened. . . .

Outside it was nearly dark. . . . A long column of brilliant orange-colored light shot skyward. . . . Our enlisted men could be seen not very far away, where, from a rather sharp rise in the ground, they were heaving sacks of something onto a fire. . . . They went about their task with the greatest glee. . . . They were having a little war all their own—a superb Fourth of July celebration—a bonfire with potato-masher hand-grenades on the side. . . . Bravo. . . .

In a deserted gun-emplacement near by they had discovered a cache of cans containing sacks of macaroni powder—the kind artillerymen use in big caliber field-pieces. . . . At first they had taken the trouble to open the cans—later they heaved the sealed cans onto the fire. . . . What sky-rockets those cans made when the heat melted the lids off and ignited the contents! One of the boys hit on the happy idea of adding a few grenades to the blaze. . . . He screwed handles into the masher-heads and pulled the fuses until this operation grew tiresome. . . . As Hosky and I arrived on the scene, the grenade-thrower pitched the remains of a box of masher-heads (it must have contained the makings of at least 75 grenades) down the hill into the gigantic bonfire. . . . In a very few moments the celebration was declared to be over, and all hands climbed into the camion headed for Laon, where we planned to spend the night. . . .

As we leisurely rolled along toward the east, we looked back occasionally. . . . There was a bright orange spot in the direction of Soissons, and once we heard the faint crack —the belated explosion of something the boys had stowed on their fire. . . . The potato-masher thrower, later known to us as the grenadier, giggled as he swung his feet over the tail of the camion and wondered what and when we would eat. . . .

An hour later we were in Laon, installed in the only hotel equipped for travellers. . . . It had been the Headquarters of the German general commanding the troops occupying the Laon vicinity. . . . The furnishings of the other hotels had been hauled away by the retreating Germans. . . .

After dinner Hosky went out on one of his characteristic scouting expeditions. . . . He returned in great excitement. . . . His discovery would not keep until morning. . . . He declared that he'd made one of the greatest finds of the war. . . . I wanted to talk to the old hotel-keeper, but Hosky insisted. . . . Together we wandered around through little dark streets—crooked streets—aimless little lonesome streets —streets that had long known the heavy tread of the blond enemy from the north and east. . . . Finally we stopped before a hole about 200 feet square. . . . Hosky assumed the rôle of a guide to Pompeii. . . .

Before one of those long-range guns of the U. S. Navy got the range of this spot, it was a moving-picture show. . . . On the particular night the navy gunners figured out the exact range it was a moving-picture show full of German officers and men, having what the French might call a "très bon evening." . . . Some fine young ensign over there in the direction of Soissons pulled the lanyard. . . . Look at the remains of the movie palace and figure out the rest of the story for yourself. . . . Moral. . . . Don't let the navy get your range. . . .

Back at the hotel we found our boys going over the camion, putting everything into shipshape for the return trip next day. . . . On examination, we found the camion to contain a very fair catch of junk—notes were made of certain things we must stock up on next day. . . .

The following morning before breakfast the old hotel-keeper told a wonderful story of the German occupation— how the Germans came in a confident rush and left in a disillusioned hurry, and on their heels that gray October day came an army of blackbirds—American negroes, part of the 370th U. S. Infantry. . . . They were on their way to

Grandloup, a near-by town to the east, where they hoped
to get another "swing" at a rapidly retreating enemy. . . .
In the past the hill city of Laon had known St. Remis, Clovis,
Queen Brunhilda, and Charlemagne, but the old hotel-
keeper didn't talk about them—he restricted himself to the
age-old enemy—the blond enemy from the east and the

LONG–RANGE NAVAL GUN

northeast. . . . How he came in a rush and left in a hurry,
and on his heels those American blackbirds. . . .

He told us of the spies who thrived in Laon during the
war . . . thrived during the four years of occupation—and
how a very spry shooting party one frosty morning in the
Bois de Vincennes paid these spies for their trouble. . . .
He apologized for the wine—the enemy had consumed the
last bottle—they had left his once famous cellar quite dry
—he knew the Pinard he served us was very bad, but he
hadn't had time to restock. . . .

Before we left town we visited the cathedral. . . . In the
square before the mediæval temple of God, Monseigneur

stood, uttering a benediction on a little group of silent wor-
shippers. . . . Monseigneur knew us at once to be Americans and gave thanks again for the coming of the blackbirds
and the French. . . .

As we started across that battle-scarred plain between
Laon and Rheims, we stopped long enough to take one more
look at the hill city. . . . The spires of the cathedral stood
out boldly against the delicate blue of the morning sky. . . .
The tiers of houses, rising one upon another, were like the
circular sections of a giant cinnamon-bun, overbrowned
from having stayed a bit too long in the oven. . . .

We lunched at Rheims—took photographs of the cathedral and Jeanne d'Arc—popped some cobwebbed corks and
took the road to Paris.

Later in the afternoon, while Hosky and I were trying to
decide on the decorative value of a German Maxim machine-
gun, one of the boys (who had been regaling himself with a
rhum-chaud in a near-by roadside café) told us that he had
just enlisted a recruit. . . . A recruit indeed! The camion
was already overloaded. . . . But, after all, a recruit was a
recruit—bring 'im out and let us look at 'im. . . . We were
advised that the recruit had ordered rhum-chauds for the
entire expedition and would bargain with us inside or not
at all. . . .

"Very well, now remember, the rhum-chauds do not come
out of expedition-funds and the camion is already overloaded. . . ."

The moment we looked at the recruit, we had visions of
courts-martial proceedings. . . . He hadn't been shaved in
"hell knew when." . . . No two parts of his uniform
matched. . . . He wore an old issue tunic, with sergeant's
stripes and a pair of breeches made of the shoddy material

issued to replacements late in the war. . . . His overseas
hat was a complete give-away. . . . All of it except half an
inch around the top was very much faded. . . . An officer's

"AND THE RHUM-CHAUDS DO NOT COME OUT OF EXPEDITION-FUNDS"—

colors had been ripped off of this half-inch, exposing the
original olive drab. . . . He spun the rarest dog-watch yarn
we had heard in some time. . . . It seems that he was a
chauffeur, detailed to drive two American officers from Paris
to Brussels. . . . This was not unusual—we had driven to
Brussels ourselves. . . . But our new-found friend had en-

countered difficulties. . . . During the night of the first day out he had been hit by something and knocked bottom side up into a shallow gully. . . .

"I wuzn't hurt, sir, not so much as to talk about—but the officers, sir, they wuz so banged about that after two weeks the doctors couldn't tell guts from gear er gizzard. . . . With the help of some passers-by, I righted the car. . . . She wouldn't run, sir, but with a little fittin' out, I slept in 'er, quite comfortable. . . . One of the officers give me 50 francs, sir, to live on till we could git straightened around. . . . I stretched it out as fur as it would go. . . . When I had only five francs left, I spent it fur a bottle of cheap hooch. . . . went out an' sat in my car an' got drunk all by myself. . . . Next day I exchanged the remains o' the car to a Frog barkeep fur value received and got drunk agin. . . . So I says to myself—well, Joe, you got drunk in it; you got drunk on it; now you hit the road and foot it. . . ."

So the recruit was really a passenger. . . . What he wanted was a free ride to Paris, where he would join his outfit. . . . The enlisted men had told him that I was a musician and kept a diary of the soldier songs I heard. . . . This was pie for Joe. . . . He would sing me a Hobo song and he did—a song about Halsted Street, Chicago—a song that was worth its weight in gold. . . .

After Joe had sung his Hobo song and the rhum-chauds had been paid for (out of expedition-funds), I gave up any idea I might have had about turning him over to the Assistant Provost Marshal when we got back to Paris. . . . The A. P. M. in Paris was a friend of mine—I had known him when he was a second lieutenant of infantry. . . . He had extracted promises from me in lieu of favors granted certain enlisted and commissioned personnel of the Air Service. . . .

But our recruit, Hobo Joe, the King of the Road, would never go to Rue St. Anne, if I had anything to say about it. . . . Joe said he didn't mind the army as long as it moved. . . . But when it stood still, he was as unhappy as a cow with a mouthful of sour grass. . . . And Joe had wounds. . . . But that's another story. . . .

We dropped our Hobo recruit off on the outskirts of Paris, near a subway-kiosk, with a click of a hundred francs and a promise to stay sober and dodge the M. P.'s. . . . (None of us took much stock in his tale about joining an outfit in Paris.) . . . It was raining as we turned off the Maux road in the direction of the Port de Fontainebleau—one of those rains that exaggerate the melodrama of Parisian nights. . . . Joe let himself down from the back of the camion, walked over to a lamp that decorated one of the street islands, pulled himself up to attention and stood at salute until we were out of sight. . . . We never saw him again. . . .

We arrived at camp about 9.30 P. M. . . . No explanations were necessary. . . . The remarkable catch of junk was a perfect alibi. . . . The German helmets were turned upside down and used as lighting-fixtures. . . . The small shell-cases were washed and used as containers for candies, nuts, and table-decorations. . . . The jazz band played behind a screen made of wicker shell-baskets—set off with garlands of mimosa, imported from the south of France. . . . A camion-load of champagne was knocked off in pledges and healths. . . .

During the party the major told me about the University plan. . . . He said I might join a group who were going to attend the Université de Lyon for the next four months. . . . He said that I might study at the Conservatoire, the Université, or wherever I liked, with full pay and allowances,

except my additional 25 per cent for flying. . . . All I had
to do was to sign my name. . . . Needless to say I signed. . . .

* * *

This is Joe's song (the tune was unimportant):

Oh, I've panhandled about Chicago town,
I've panhandled from Halsted Street to Puget Sound,
I've fingered the roll and made many a click. . . .
But never used a jimmy ur a loaded stick.

Chorus:
Oh, it's hit the road, you lousy bums,
You stiffs and weary Willies.
You walk and sleep, you sit and doze,
You hooligans and tillies.
For tho' you've worked the Central,
The Katy, and the Soo,
There's no place like Chicago
For bums like me and you.

Now, when it's spring in Halsted Street
And you get the itching in yer feet,
There's always pimps with lots o' kale
Fur scabbin' jobs they got fur sale.

Chorus:
Oh, it's hit the road, etc.

Sometimes in Halsted Street it's hot,
But up in Soo country it's not;
And there ain't no bulls nur coppers there
To beat your wangle and give yu the air.

Chorus:
Oh, it's hit the road, etc.

Oh, lemme have a skin full o' good red booze
An' I'm king o' the road till I walk out o' my shoes,

'Cause I never spilled a squeal nur lightened half on a touch
Nur let a bozo bo hang high and dry in dutch.

Chorus:

Oh, it's hit the road, etc.

Now, when I lay my bones to rest
Bury me with the hobos I like the best—
Jack, the Lifter, Frank, and one-eyed Ed. . . .
Bury me with my pardners when I'm dead.

Chorus:

Oh, it's hit the road, etc.

For tho' we're scabby and lousy and old,
The truth of our miseries has never been told.
We wangle fur a little and touch a lot less
And damn seldom clik much real happiness.

Chorus:

Oh, it's hit the road, etc.

CHAPTER VI

IN Lyon, six of us—five aviation officers and a lieutenant of artillery—moved into an apartment in the Rue des Ramparts d'Ainy. The French woman who owned the apartment and her servants remained and became responsible for the table, the general caretaking, etc. We lived like princes—breakfasts in bed—lunches and dinners served in the grand manner, with appropriate wines and liqueurs. When our hostess ran out of anything, such as sugar or coffee, we procured it at a very low rate from our commissary. Indeed, we lived on the fat of the land.

We were supposed to go to school—some of us did, but, as a rule, we toured France—southern France, the Rhone Valley, or the country off to the left in the direction of Aix les Bains, the Italian frontier, or Switzerland. It was a hard war—that battle of Lyon (Rhone).

We had been in Lyon but a few days when I was reminded of the death and burial of a flying-partner of mine—a boy from a very fine family out in the States—the same boy who planned to give me the address of his sweetheart while we were at sea on the old *Covington*. His mother wrote me from London—soon she would arrive. She had come from a town in Ohio. She intended to visit the grave of her son. I had helped him die, but that's not an easy thing to explain to a mother. He had fallen a victim to his own imaginings—he had brought about his own death through picturing himself "bounced off."

One evening in the early fall of 1918, I suggested a hair-cut for both of us—a really high-class French hair-cut, with lotions, perfumes, tonics, etc.

"Hair-cut, hell. Come on, boy, I'll spend the money on some good drinkin' liquor. Hair-cuts don't become aviators, anyway. Why, I'm going to be bounced off in a few days—what's the use of wasting the money on French barbers!"

And now his mother would soon be in Paris. She would rest there a while and then visit the grave of her son—if I would help her find it.

About two weeks before the crash, he'd given me the address of his sweetheart—but the discreet answer to my note was signed by a married woman. Strange! A year seemed to be a long time in the life of war-time love.

Soon now his mother would be in Paris. I would be granted leave. We would visit the grave (if I could find it). She would shed a few tears, take some pictures. I would recite the tellable details of her son's army life. And she would return to her home in Ohio.

We had been hedge-hopping, in spite of a ground mist, when he took the top off a brick chimney with the under-carriage of his plane. I had trouble finding a place to land—vineyards, haystacks, and cut-up fields everywhere. When I did get back to the place where he had fallen, some ambulance-men from a near-by anti-aircraft emplacement had taken charge of his remains. He had died a few moments after falling.

Colored boys made up the burial squad. The aviator was the last detail of the day. Burial squads (made up of colored boys) never worked at night—never! I might have got away before dark, but I heard part of a song sung by one of the grave-diggers. He sang about having a "grave-diggin' feelin'"' in his heart. I remained and took it down in detail.

The smashed airplane had caught fire. By nightfall only a heap of tangled, grayish wreckage remained—tanks—interplane wires—the metal parts of the undercarriage—strut fittings—the aileron controls—and the engine, from which a thin column of gray smoke slowly trickled skyward.

This is the song the boys sang as they worked at burying the fallen aviator:

> I've got a grave-diggin' feelin' in my heart—
> I've got a grave-diggin' feelin' in my heart—
> I shivers and shakes in my soul—
> When I looks in dat big black hole—
> I've got a grave-diggin' feelin' in my heart.
>
> I've got a grave-diggin' feelin' in my heart—
> I've got a grave-diggin' feelin' in my heart—
> Don't bury dose boys so deep in de ground—
> Dey has to hear Gabriel's reveille sound—
> I've got a grave-diggin' feelin' in my heart.
>
> I've got a grave-diggin' feelin' in my heart—
> I've got a grave-diggin' feelin' in my heart—
> When I looks in dat grave I gets me a chill—
> 'Cause I knows if I gets in, I has to stay until—
> I've got a grave-diggin' feelin' in my heart.
>
> I've got a grave-diggin' feelin' in my heart—
> I've got a grave-diggin' feelin' in my heart—
> Everybody died in de A. E. F.,
> Only one burial squad wuz left'—
> I've got a grave-diggin' feelin' in my heart.

And now it's springtime of another year. The Frenchman has repaired his chimney and there are flowers in every hedgerow. Soon to the legend of the fallen aviator will be added the visit of the mother, who came from her home in Ohio to visit the grave of her son.

* * *

I'VE GOT A GRAVE-DIGGIN' FEELIN' IN MY HEART

(In the notes of this song, I find the word "notion" used with the word "feeling." The notes, however, are very indistinct, and it may be the word "notion" was written on the sheet before I took down the details of the song.)

GRAVE–DIGGERS

I got a grave - dig - gin' feel - in' in my

heart; I got a grave - dig - gin' feel - in' in my

heart. I shiv - ers and shakes in my soul

When I looks in dat big black hole. I got a
grave - dig-gin' feel - in' in my heart.

LYON (RHONE), FRANCE—SPRINGTIME—1919

"Bin? Bin? Boy, I'se done bin. An' I'm goin' back—
as soon as dis here ghost act is over. You can burn my
spiral putties. But, boy, I was seein' double. Four flights
under de sidewalk—Cut my throat! What a jamboree!
Dey calls it 'De Celestian Bar.'"

"Aw, hell! Ain't no such thing—it's 'De Café des
Célestines'!"

"Pouff you—café! Hell! You wouldn't know a café if
you wuz to see one. Listen, Bugboy, dat's a bar—and what's
more, it's a 'celestial bar.'"

"How'd you git in dat place? How'd you find it?"

"I went wid a couple a frog friends o' mine and dis here high yellow boy what takes care of baggage. And did we

walk de dog? Cut my throat! Did we walk de dog! Why, man, dey passed out refreshments I ain't never tasted since I been put here. An' all I did this mornin' was to drink a glass o' water, and boy howdy! I was pres-i-dent of France."

They were making up in the back rooms of an unused

Café Chantant. The theatre and the café were set in the middle of a very charming little garden on the outskirts of Lyon. The Y. M. C. A. had taken over the Café in order to properly house the travelling army shows.

These army shows were the result of an almost divine hunch. They were immensely amusing—they diverted the minds of boys who could not go home (for lack of ship-space), gave others something to do, and even developed talent that might never have seen the light of day.

The performance we witnessed on this particular night opened with the often used jazz band and dribbled through a rather bad lot of worn-out buffoonery. They did the old sentry act—an American private walking post. He carries an old short-barrelled rifle with a length of rubber hose slipped down over the end. As he walks, this length of hose waves up and down in the rhythm of his gait. It is supposed to be night. Some one approaches.

"Halt! Who goes there?"

"Troisième batallon mitrailleuse—j'ai carte d'identité.

"Pass, Frog!"

Another is halted.

"Well, now, I say, my dear fellow, is it really in order for one to tell one's name?"

"Pass, Limey!"

Another attempts to pass.

"Halt! Who goes there "

"Who the hell wants to know?"

"Pass, Yank!"

But we had applauded this before.

Then, though we didn't know it, the thing we had been waiting for all evening happened—the Ghost Act—ten negroes, one soloist and nine singing ensemble. They represented the ghosts of boys who had been bounced off in the war. They were costumed like members of the Ku Klux Klan. The effect was excellent—white shrouds—blue lights —sepulchral voices. The soloist stepped forward and confidentially sang one line to the audience.

My mama told me not to come over here—

Then the ensemble joined the singing:

But I did, I did, I did.

The soloist continued:

My mama said they surely would shoot me dead—
An' they did, they did, they did. . . .
I tried to keep my secret from every shot and shell—
But 'long come one that made me tell. . . .

The entire group concluding with:

My mama told me not to come over here,
But I did, I did, I did.

Other verses:

My papa tole me not to come over here,
But I did, I did, I did,
My papa said not for me to get myself shot,
But I did, I did, I did.
Draft come along—in I went,
When de war got hot I was sent. . . .
My papa told me not to come over here,
But I did, I did, I did.

My pastor told me not to come over here,
But I did, I did, I did,

He said, "Now, Sam, they surely will get your ham,"
An' they did, they did, they did. . . .
When de whole German army passed over my head—
I knew I was lyin' on my death bed. . . .
My pastor told me not to come over here,
But I did, I did, I did.

Nothing short of pandemonium broke loose—men yelled
—girls screamed—French visitors, not understanding one
word of this strange funereal procedure, were decidedly
frightened. The song was, of course, repeated—with almost
the same results. If the Café des Célestines had not been
calling so loudly, the performance might have gone on all
night. I am convinced that this song produced one of the
best laughs of the war.

Odd-shaped little patches of moonlight fell from the edges
of buildings as we turned to go back into the city. Crossing
the Rhone we could see the grayish white of the new President Wilson bridge—faintly outlined against a lead-colored
background. The river scarcely seemed to move at all. Re-
flecting the lights from the bridges, it was more like oil be-
sprinkled with fireflies. Place Bellecour was quiet—the
flower-stands had their windows fastened down—the Pa-
villon d'Orchestre was dark. Far across the top of the spires
and chimney-pots we could distinguish a faint light in the
tower of the Observatoire, and, higher up the hill, Notre
Dame de Fourvière—"like a fairy-palace hanging in the
sky."

There had been a promise of dancing in the Y. M. C. A.
Canteen in the Place Carnot. It proved to be only a promise. The jazz band was there, but there were no dancing
partners. The jazz band of eight players (all colored) did
their stuff, dance or no dance,—and how they did mourn

GHOST SONG

Arranged by J. J. N.

My ma - ma told me not to come o - ver here, but

I did, I did, I did. My ma - ma said they sure-ly

would shoot me dead, and they did, they did, they did.   I

tried to keep my se-cret from ev-ery shot and shell, but

'long come one that made me tell. Oh, my ma-ma told me not to

come o-ver here, but I did, I did, I did.

through those blue Midnight Blues! All the boys except the banjoist would stop now and then and sing to the banjo's droning "chum-e-um-chum-chum." The pianist sounded off

about having some wrinkles in his empty belly. We gathered up a collection of five-franc notes—"presented" them to the leader, and started to take our leave. The colored boys were overjoyed at our token of appreciation—they would do one more tune and "call it a day." The banjoist struck a chord —and a superbly balanced double quartette sang unaccompanied:

JAIL HOUSE

ARRANGED BY J. J. N.

Pa-pa's in de jail house from shoot-in' of de dice.

Sher - iff told 'im once but he would-n't tell 'im twice, So

pa - pa's in de jail house now.

Verse

I don't want to do no

more K. P.   Pa - pa's in de jail house

now.   Ser - geant, won't you have a lit - tle

pit - y on me,   Pa-pa's in de jail house now.   Oh,

D. C.

Chorus:

Papa's in de jail house from shootin' of de dice—
Sheriff told 'im once but he wouldn't tell 'im twice,
So—papa's in de jail house now.

Oh, I don't want to do no more K. P.,
'Cause papa's in de jail house now. . . .
Mr. Sergeant, won't you have a little pity on me?
'Cause papa's in de jail house now.

Papa's in de jail house from shootin' of de dice,
Sheriff told 'im once but he wouldn't tell 'im twice,
So—papa's in de jail house now.

Goin' to take my shirt to swab out my gun. . . .
'Cause papa's in de jail house now. . . .
Hope to shoot a hole in a nice fat Hun. . . .
'Cause papa's in de jail house now.

Papa's in de jail house from shootin' of de dice,
Sheriff told him once but he wouldn't tell 'im twice,
So—papa's in de jail house now.

I found a nail in my corn beef—
Papa's in de jail house now—
My belly'll turn me into a thief—
'Cause papa's in de jail house now.

Papa's in de jail house from shootin' of de dice,
Sheriff told him once but he wouldn't tell 'im twice,
So—papa's in de jail house now.

Goin' to send my girl a souvenir,
'Cause papa's in de jail house now—
It'll be some German major's ear,
'Cause papa's in de jail house now.

Papa's in de jail house from shootin' of de dice,
Sheriff told 'im once but he wouldn't tell 'im twice,
So—papa's in de jail house now.

The arrival of a group of colored soldiers who were ex-
tolling the Café des Célestines in unnecessarily loud voices
reminded us that these boys had to take the night train to
Dijon in order to play their engagement next day. We saw
them last as they clambered sleepily across the Place Carnot
in the direction of the railway-station, the bass-fiddle player
bringing up the rear, like some fantastic somebody in a fairy
tale, making a quick getaway with a fabulous bag of plunder.

* * *

CARNIVAL IN THE VALLEY OF THE RHONE

The score of l'Enfant Prodigue was on the piano-shelf before me. My fingers played through Debussy's lovely pas-
sages, but my mind was far away. It was Carnival in the
Valley of the Rhone. Vagabondia had the best of me. I had
visions of a broad river flowing majestically past mediæval
cities—Avignon, Tarascon, Arles, Beaucaire, Villeneuve les
Avignon. The walls of my studio in the Rue du Platre
leaned in at the top. Pass or no pass, I had to go—to-
morrow, for sure—perhaps, even, to-night. Would I ask for
a pass? Passes involved military police. The lack of passes
might involve courts martial. Why not give up my uniform and go as a civilian! My friend the "Purveyor to

Renegades" would help me. He would outfit me as a French civilian. I would stay two weeks if I had luck—two spring-time weeks in Provence—two weeks of Carnival in the Valley of the Rhone.

Men from all walks of life made up the United States Army—men from the best families—from the greatest universities—from the shops—from the hills—from the farms. It was impossible to assemble two million men and not have it so. They were not the kind of people who lend themselves to "big-stick" methods. Some tin-hat higher-up failed to make this discovery—that's why so many men came home cursing the service—and still curse it. That's why nearly all Military Police (except marines) were so unpopular. Marines have military policing down to such a science.

My friend the "purveyor to renegades" was, among other things, a socialist. The trade he carried on was not particularly an illegal one—he merely supplied you with a costume. You paid in advance and left your own clothing as a deposit. He had a room full of mail-boxes. One might receive one's mail at his establishment for ten francs by the year. The patrons of this branch of the business were mostly females. Then there was the information department (which, very possibly, bordered onto a blackmailing service), and, finally, a directory of names and addresses. The business was carried on under the guileless name of a "public bath-house." Indeed, there were a few baths—and a private bar. What I feared most was that the authorities would end the career of this "public benefactor" while my uniform was on deposit. This might lead to complications. Nevertheless, that night I was on my way—travelling as a civilian. Early the next morning I was far down the valley of the Rhone—there were wild strawberries, blooming in the fence corners and on

the sides of the roads—fraises au bois—violets, flowering
shrubs, and fruit-trees. For it was Carnival—Carnival, indeed, in the Valley of the Rhone.

I had come part of the way on the P. L. M., walked a bit,
and concluded the journey by water. The Rhone was a
silent river that morning—its silvery colored surface chang-
ing now and again into odd-shaped multicolored patches, as
if oil had been poured upon it. Approaching Avignon from
the river is like turning a corner suddenly and finding one-
self staring at the setting of some mediæval play, which the
stage-hands of the fourteenth century had forgotten to
strike. There, against the sky, that was more like a cyclo-
rama than a sky, stood Notre Dame des Doms and the Palace of the Popes. I was far enough away to lose the effect
of square corners—it was a mighty ensemble of spires and
belfries—of battlements—of turrets and towers—where the
rhythmic sweep of long lines had not been broken into by
useless embellishments. I thought how the Church might
be likened to a spider, carrying the makings of its lair on its
back, weaving, as it went, a well-nigh imperishable web.

The next three days were spent between Avignon and
Villeneuve. I was about to take off in the direction of Tarascon, when a young lady with very black, insinuating eyes
suggested that I should remain for a performance of music
—a benefit concert. The playing of a violinist who had won
prizes in the past would be the principal attraction. He
would play on a very fine old violin loaned to him for the
performance.

The effect upon me was inexplicable—it may have been
the sheer beauty of the Cesar Franck Sonata—it may have
been the summed-up effect of my three days spent in the
faded splendor of mediæval cities. It was most possibly be-

cause the violinist had found out how to play. The war had taught him to give up playing notes—he was translating ideas. He paused a long time before he began to play— then I heard phrases of music like the sighing of the wind through snow-encrusted pines—sobbing tones, echoing, answering—faintly blending with the tone of the piano—swirling—spinning—disappearing. I closed my eyes, that I might listen more closely.

My imagination bridged the six hundred years between the Avignon of to-day and the Avignon of the popes. I saw the pageantry of the fourteenth century—Phillip the Fair, King of France—the two popes named Clement—Pope John, the shoemaker's son—Benedict—Innocent—Urban—and, finally, Gregory, who carried the Holy See back to Rome.

There was a pause—the violinist tuned—the music continued. He was playing a more virile movement now. In my imagination there were shell-swept villages, jagged buildings, limbless trees, rutted roads plainly showing the deeply marked tracks of caterpillar wheels—a group of crosses in a poppy-skirted grain-field. From one of the crosses hangs an olive-drab helmet. My eyes were full of twilight, but my soul was sailing in a fairy-ship—a fairy-ship made of catgut, curly maple, ebony, and horsehair. I knew that divine fingers were racing to catch each quirk and turn of a far diviner pen. I felt myself sinking under an avalanche of exquisite sounds.

As I dusted the twilight from my eyes, I began to see the men who made a part of this supreme expression—John Sebastian Bach, who gave us the tempered scale; an Italian fiddle-maker, perhaps the fiddle-maker of Cremona; Paganini, who raised the art of fiddle-playing to the task of a god; Eugene Ysaye, for whom the sonata had been written; a soldier, who had discovered the divinity of expression, a soldier in the costume of an artilleryman; and a modest little man who had objectified his dreams into a most glorious sonata—Cesar Franck.

I spent the remainder of that magical night wandering about—indulging myself in great deep breaths of the perfume-laden night air, listening to the silken rustle of young cypress and willow leaves—listening to the voice of the night-bird, as he confided his tale to the sleepy-eyed, dew-heavy flowers. For Provence is the land of the nightingale.

Passing through Tarascon, Beaucaire, Arles, Montmajor, les Beaux, and Orange was like walking in a dream. My two weeks had nearly expired. Time had been overbalanced by the legends of the Courts of Love, Good King René, Aucassin and Nicolette. I had sat in Roman arenas and rubbed shoulders with some beautiful yesterdays.

At Vienne (a small town, not far from Lyon) I made my last stop. It was long past dark when I arrived at the railway-station to inquire about trains going north. On the dimly lighted platform I saw a group of soldiers. The fact that I was without the law (being out of uniform and having only a three-day pass) had led me to avoid the military. Would it be possible that I would be detected so near the end of my journey! I stood in the darkest place I could find and waited.

"Yes, and he wuz black. An' he wuz soldierin' like we is. How come he cou'nt compree our parlez-vous?"

I was safe. They were American negro soldiers, who had lost their way. For fear they should recognize me, I talked as little as possible and made my English sound as French as I knew how. They took me for a guide who had learned a smattering of English, in order to profit by the business of

travelling Americans after the war. The negroes had intended to go to St. Étienne. A French negro (who, of course,
could not understand one word of English) had advised them
to get off ten kilometres too soon.

"An' boy, I'll write my name on dat African, ef ever I
sees 'im agin."

"No, you won't write yo' name on 'im. Hugh-ugh! Not
unless he gits palsy er St. Peter's two-step all of a sudden-
like, an' can't whip out dat blade he wuz a totin'. Why, lad,
did you see his corn-knife? Can't you see dat African bein'
a nasty bastard when he goes to swingin' dat blade promis-
cuous?"

The station-agent could not be found, but a grizzled old
fellow who seemed to be the guard over the freight and
baggage-house told me that a train would pass about midnight, and it would make connections with the line running
to St. Étienne. The black men were pacified by the news
of another train. One of them, a burly, heavy-set fellow,
sang out on the night air:

> Roll, Jordan, roll—roll, Jordan, roll—
> Soldier, you'll be called on,
> To shake that thing you're settin' on,
> Dey's a battle bein' fought in de Argonne,
> Roll, Jordan, roll.

"Say, Elephant Iron, you'd bes' pipe down. It's time mos'
gentry is thinkin' more 'bout sleepin' dan singin'. If you
must sing, keep it down a bit. Whar' you headin' fur, Mr.
French Man?"

"Moi? Je vais à Lyon.'

"Oh, you a goin' to Lyon! We is powerful obliged to you
fur findin' out 'bout de train. I can't talk enough French
to tell you, but you compree, we merci you a lot."

I almost said something like "Oh, don't mention it," which would have been fatal. Elephant Iron (so named, no doubt, from the deep wrinkle in the side of his face), was at it again—

> Roll, Jordan, roll—roll, Jordan, roll—
> Pastor, you'll be called on—
> To help some soldier pass on,
> 'Cause he's never goin' to fight in de Argonne,
> Roll, Jordan, roll.

The others joined in, a few at a time, until the ensemble reminded me of a hay-wagon load of merrymakers returning from a day in the country. They were singing, not because they wanted to, but rather because they couldn't keep from it. Their spokesman (who appeared to be the leading spirit) took up a song that I knew at once to be a camp-meeting tune from the States. The first verse was sung so softly I missed the words—the refrain came out more clearly.

> Pray for forgiveness, pray for forgiveness—
> Pray for forgiveness—
> Dat's all de po' black sinner can do.

The remainder of the song was easily taken down. The melancholy manner of their singing touched me. Had fortune favored these colored men with a musical education? If ten per cent of them had been through grammar-school, fortune had smiled, indeed. Yet here was an unaffected musical performance that more than compared with the violin-playing I had heard in Avignon. If those colored boys had known that I understood them and was at that moment writing down their song, they might have gone to showing

This is the song Elephant Iron sang.

ROLL, JORDAN, ROLL

ARRANGED BY J. J. N.

Roll, Jordan, roll. Roll, Jordan, roll. Soldier, you'll be called on To

shake that thing your sit - tin' on. There's a bat - tle be - in'

fought in de Ar - gonne. Roll, Jor - dan, roll.

off, as I had seen others do so often. But I'd caught them, for once, unawares.

> Debil works by night and by day—
> But de blood of de Lamb will wash yo' sins away,
> If you'll pray for forgiveness, pray for forgiveness—
> Pray for forgiveness,
> Dat's all de poor black sinner can do.

Why will the negro, who is thought of as a happy person, revert to such sad ideas in his singing! The negro has no so-called love-songs. He adopts musical motifs from the whites near at hand and energizes them with the yearnings of his soul. Some folks have said that the negro finds happiness through self-commiseration. This is not altogether true. The constant recurring note of sadness in the music of the black man is like the ripple of a stream of water running around a rock—the water being his thought-stream—the rock, suppression.

In Paris the Peace Conference was in session. Nations, not having found out that "thought" is the only causative power in the universe, were trying to bring about peace by treaties. They were preparing a mixture known as the "safety of nations." They would apply this mixture with a wide brush. Next spring the early rains would wash the mixture off and a new batch would have to be mixed and applied. How far away all this seemed! I was listening to the singing of angels.

> Night comes out when de sun goes down—
> But de poor black sinner has to wander around
> An' pray for forgiveness, pray for forgiveness,
> Pray for forgiveness—
> Dat's all de poor black sinner can do.

Sarajevo—the Dardanelles—the freedom of the seas—the Bagdad Railway—the security of lesser nations—how far away all that seemed! President Wilson knew that war came from the inner emotions of man—that nations had to think peace before they could objectify it into reality. Clemenceau and Lloyd George knew that peace was not an external something, dependent on silly political rivalries. And Cardinal Mercier (a man sent of God if ever there was one) had made this thought the basis of one of his immortal utterances. But the nations wanted signed documents. Therefore the treaty.

> Oh, de mule he can bray and de whippoorwill can sing—
> But de poor black sinner can't do a thing,
> But pray for forgiveness, pray for forgiveness—
> Pray for forgiveness—
> Dat's all de poor black sinner can do.

So—in Paris the Peace Conference held forth. The delegates were stringing out the conferences. They were practising the old diplomatic trick of keeping the world on the threshold of hope—not depending on the gratitude of the boorish constituents—because hope has an excellent memory—while gratitude has none at all.

And all the while, the cafés in Montmartre were full of intoxicated American news-writers—news-writers, secretaries, stenographers, and adventurers—loud-mouthed Americans showing the French how to spend their evenings. In the Champs Élysées olive-drab limousines whizzed by—they carried ladies and gentlemen in evening dress—olive-drab staff-cars, whizzing by soldiers and civilians on foot—soldiers and civilians with vague feelings of unrest. How far away all this seemed!

The colored boys had got around to the inevitable "lonesome" song:

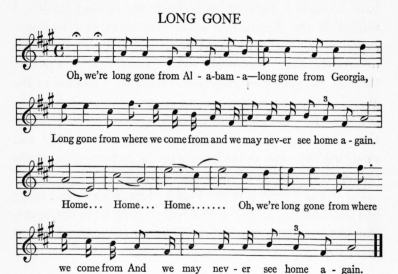

LONG GONE

Oh, we're long gone from Al - a-bam - a—long gone from Georgia,

Long gone from where we come from and we may nev-er see home a - gain.

Home... Home... Home....... Oh, we're long gone from where

we come from And we may nev - er see home a - gain.

Oh, we're long gone from Alabama—long gone from Georgia,
Long gone from where we come from and we may never see
　　home again.
Home—home—home—Oh, we're long gone from where we
　　come from—
And we may never see home again.

Oh, de whippoorwill's a singin' low and de cotton's in de
　　pod—
But many of us is goin' to rest, beneath dis far-off sod.
Oh, we're long gone from Alabama, long gone from Georgia,
Long gone from North Carolina, and we may never see home
　　again.

A train of dimly lighted cars stopped at the station. The
negroes were still singing (a verse I did not record) when

they climbed into a sparsely populated coach. I missed the train deliberately—why go back to Lyon! At least, why go back to-night? Turning away from the railway-station, I walked in the direction of some Roman ruins I had seen earlier in the day. A belated moon was shining—the moon of strawberries. Its feeble light cast fantastic shadows through the gently moving trees—shadows I likened to the ghosts of Cæsar's legions making merry, as they did on the eve of battle—the ghosts of Cæsar's legions, reclining on the tiers of a beautiful new arena, nudging one another and smacking their lips at the beauty of the dancing girls, in the first century version of the Folies Bergère.

For it was Carnival in the Valley of the Rhone, and fancy had deceived me so well that I had rescued from my countless score of days two delicious weeks—two weeks I had spent listening to the singing of the angels.

* * *

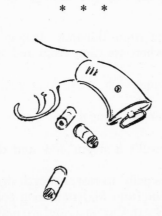

PRAY FOR FORGIVENESS

ARRANGED BY J. J. N.

De mule he can bray and de whip-por-will can sing, But de

poor black sin - ners can't do a thing But pray for for -

give - ness, pray for for - give - ness; Pray for for-

give - - ness, dat's all de poor black sin-ners can do.

CHAPTER VII

THE Battle of Lyon was over the morning of July 1, 1919—both sides claiming a victory. . . . One American had taken unto himself an American wife—a local Y. M. C. A. girl. . . . Two Americans had nearly taken unto themselves a French wife each. . . . A lack of birth-certificates halted the consummation of the Anglo-French nuptials until safely after train time. . . . There were various rumors of other "affairs du cœur." . . . Some of the fiancées had gone so far as to send the mothers of their American lovers gifts of hand-made underthings—gifts which, after all, didn't seem to make much of a hit with the prospective mothers-in-law.

The souvenir-collectors among us left town with a goodly load of bad etchings and fake antique clay pottery. . . . A few of our boys actually carried away certificates, showing the completion of certain courses of study at the Université de Lyon. . . . Several sat back on their haunches and refused to leave town—having, perhaps, better judgment than they were given credit for at the time. . . . Everything considered, it was an exciting morning—July the first, 1919.

Five of the officers carried blank passes. . . . We might have filled them out for Afghanistan, Tibet, Indo-China, or Tahiti, and still have been within the law. . . . We were, in fact, supposed to be headed for the port of Brest—wherever that was . . . Brest, France . . . Camp Pontanazen, etc. . . . Two of us started immediately for Issoudun. . . . Before leaving Lyon, a certain group had planned to meet in the Central Post-Office at Brest, France, at high noon, July the 10th. . . . This gave us a margin of nine days to sight-see about in France and Germany, A. W. O. L.

At Issoudun we were received by our French friends as long-lost brothers—received—wined—dined and entertained in truly grand style. . . . We visited the flying-field. . . . Grass had grown up in the roads. . . . The Red Cross Canteen, once so full of familiar faces, was falling into ruin. . . . The canvas sides of empty airplane-hangars flapped idly in the breeze. . . . One heard the aimless banging of barracks-doors and was reminded of haunted houses.

The doors and windows of *The Plane News* office were open. . . . The wind had scattered the remains of the last edition a hundred metres in all directions. . . . The floor of the editor's office was covered with notes, data, cancelled copy, proof-sheets, old editions, etc. . . . We took a few pictures of the graveyard and left hurriedly—in very low spirits.

Next morning we were in Paris. . . . The same night in Liége. . . . July the Fourth found us in Cologne, Germany. . . . From Cologne we went to Brussels and then to Antwerp, where we stopped long enough to plan an invasion into Holland. . . . The tale of how we coerced an American colonel into issuing the orders that took us to Holland twice in one week is a story all by itself. . . . And that Holland trip!—punctuated with Rembrandt, antique Spanish architecture, gin, The Hague, inquisitions, the Queen, Schevening, glazed pottery, the seaside, etc., etc., etc. . . . That Holland trip was an A. W. O. L. high spot.

The 14th of July, 1919, everybody on the Continent who could afford a ticket to Paris and find a place on the Champs Élysées watched the first real display the Parisians had staged since the 11th of November, 1918. . . . A few days

later we arrived in Brest. . . . Our appointment on July
10th was, of course, long passed. . . . It happened that
none of the others were really there, although most of them
claimed to have been. . . . Brest was, in the language of
the negro, "our last go round," and it came near to being
the dullest "go round" of the whole war.

We had, with some fear and trembling, just presented our
orders—our orders and the trumped-up passes. . . . A colored boy approached us from the kitchen of a near-by mess.
. . . He was wearing a smile much like a slice of watermelon.

"Hello, Lieutenant Johnston. . . . How come you're
here? . . . Boy, howdy, I knows you remembers me . . .
I'm Harry . . . I used to work at de Santa Fe railway-
station."

He was saluting with both hands.

"Yes, Harry, I do remember you—surely, I do."

"Yessir, I worked fo' your daddy, too. . . . Off 'n'on-like.
. . . Course we didn't quit friends . . . nossar . . . not
'zakly."

"So you joined the army?"

"Nossar, I didn't jine—de man at de court-house jined
fur me."

"Well, tell me, Harry, how long have you been in France?"

"Lemme see—next come July, it'll be a year."

"Why, it's already July."

"Sho' nuf? It's a year if it's July. . . . And I been all
over."

He gave the names of a dozen French villages all within
10 kilometres of Brest.

"How big a camp is Brest? How many men do you suppose they have here?"

"Well, now, lieutenant, I just disremembers fur de moment. . . . I don't know if dey is six thousand or six million. . . . Yessar, Brest is a wow of a camp . . . A wow!"

All the tours of inspection conceived in the mind of man could not have found out all about Brest. . . . It was a port of mysteries. . . . The story has been told, after a fashion, and will be told again. . . . The story of the stone barracks built by Napoleon, surrounded by a city of wooden barracks and tents built by the United States—the duckboards over the perpetual mud-puddles—delousing and fumigating plants—laundries—mess-halls—hospitals—a war-brides'* camp—the water-front—the drowsy harbor full of transports—the French navy-yards with their huge dry-docks—the warehouses full of unmarked army baggage—the grog-shops—the fights between sailors, military police, and soldiers. . . . What a grab-bag for the writers of the future!

We hadn't been in Brest an hour when we were called up for a physical examination. . . . It looked like mosquito-bites. . . . The doctor was of a different opinion.

"What are yu doin' for the itch, lieutenant?"

"Why, hell, we're scratchin' it like everybody else."

"Don't seem to do it much good, does it? I mean scratching."

"Well, not a hell of a lot."

"All right—now—er—just go over there between those two guards and——"

---

* At a good safe distance from the main camp at Brest, the United States Army had established a so-called War-Brides' Camp. . . . It was a separate little command within a command, hidden so well that only a few of us morbid curiosity-seekers ever found it. . . . The brides were kept segregated during the daytime, being permitted to entertain their respective husbands after the evening meal. . . . This was done in a little wooded section of French countryside, under the eyes of a sentry who walked post and tried to maintain order as nearly as possible. . . . Knowing American soldiers and Continental brides, one can easily imagine the difficulty of this assignment. . . . Female welfare workers told us some rare tales about the life of the war-brides inside their barracks—their scraps at meal-time—the smashed dishes—the hair-pullings, etc. . . .

The guards very obligingly led us off to the contagious skin-disease camp. . . . Our clothes were taken away from us and carefully marked. . . . Then we were shown a tent where an odd collection of unfortunates, stricken like ourselves, were playing poker, shooting craps, rubbing their bodies with a grease containing coarsely powdered sulphur —and cursing their luck generally. . . . For the next seventy-two hours we did the same. . . . And then a bath. . . . The itch was gone.

A laundry was operated in connection with the bathhouse. . . . Here, from a little square window, a colored boy handed us our deloused, laundered, and chemically clean-smelling clothing. . . . As he did so, he sang:

CLEAN CLOTHES SONG

Clean clothes for clean boys; Not a bug, not an itch,

Not a louse nor an-y sich; Step up, lads, an' git 'em.

Second Version

Clean clothes for clean boys; Coot-ies gone, fleas all dead,

Ev-ery-thing is clean in-stead. Clean clothes

for clean boys; Step up, lads, an' git 'em.

> Clean clothes for clean boys—
> Not a bug—not an itch—
> Not a louse nur any sich. . . .
> Clean clothes for clean boys—
> Step up, lads, and git 'em.

Here was a boy who had invented his own working song. . . . Not that he did so much singing—it seemed to be more like the buzz of a summer-tired locust. . . .

> Clean clothes for clean boys—
> Cooties* gone—fleas dead—
> Eveything clean instead. . . .
> Clean clothes for clean boys—
> Step up, lads, and git 'em.

That night there were prize-fights. . . . The preliminaries included a "battle-royal." . . . It proved to be the kind of battle-royal I had often seen in the South—fifteen colored boys turned loose in the ring—each the mortal enemy of the other. . . . What a slugging-match that was. . . . The prize was 25 francs—about 4 dollars. . . . As we left the ringside, the voice of a colored boy raised itself above the noise of the crowd:

"Not me—nossar—not dis chicken. . . . I won't git myself cooled fur nobody's 25 francs. . . . Nossar—not me."

But the *Northern Pacific*, the *Cap Finistère*, the *Zeppelin*, and other seagoing tugs were in the harbor. . . . The *Northern Pacific* drew so little water that she could be

---

* Some boys were never bothered by lice, cooties, or other vermin. . . . Others could find a louse or a flea most any time—particularly a flea. . . . We had in our outfit at one time a lad known as "dumb John"—(he had such a dumb look on his face, one could see it in the dark)—who never failed to find a flea whenever he wanted to. . . .

brought up 'longside. . . . The others had to stand off 500 metres or so in the deeper water of the harbor.

Gangs of stevedores had been working far into the night, loading foot-lockers, bags, and boxes into their holds. . . . By a special permit we had been admitted to the dock on which the baggage-warehouse stood. . . . My friends must be sure their baggage went aboard (if it could be found). . . . A long-legged friend of mine had told me of a song the stevedores sometimes sang about Georgia. . . . My interest in baggage was only secondary.

It was late when we arrived at the pier. . . . A bronzy looking August moon hung lopsidedly in the east. . . . Water-soaked hawsers tightened and slackened with the almost imperceptible movements of the steamer. . . . The sound of metal-rubbing wood came from up forward. . . . It was a slow, rasping sound—like badly produced notes on a bass fiddle.

Some sailor-men, off duty for a few hours, were loafing on the outboard side of the warehouse. . . . Sailor-men loafing, singing in the unnatural cigarette-voice so often heard.

DESTROYER SONG

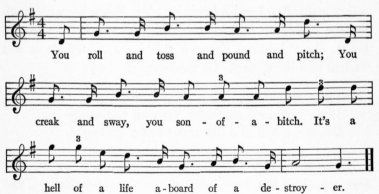

You roll and toss and pound and pitch; You creak and sway, you son - of - a - bitch. It's a hell of a life a-board of a de - stroy - er.

You roll and toss and pound and pitch—
You creak and sway, you son-of-a-bitch. . . .
It's a hell of a life aboard of a destroyer.

Oh, we've heard tales of trenches told—
Tales of cooties fierce and bold. . . .
But we've our bedbugs in the hold. . . .
It's a hell of a life aboard of a destroyer.

In order to present the bedbug in a musical setting, they
had to distort the original form of the song from four to five
measures. . . . This didn't seem to matter at all. . . .
They even repeated the bedbug-couplet to demonstrate their
utter disregard for such a trifle as form in music.

Turning from the bedbug, they promptly began to tell the
real truth about "life aboard of a destroyer," employing
much unprintable matter and referring to many very re-
volting operations. . . . This was by no means the Georgia
song—the one I had hoped to hear. . . . My partners were
busy rummaging in great piles of baggage—I joined them
and waited.

A short coffin (one end had rotted off in a Q. M. store-
house) contained most of my treasures. . . . Then there
was a bed-roll, a foot-locker, etc. . . . While we were read-
ing the names on endless rows of ill-shapen duffle-bags and
boxes, the stevedores changed shifts. . . . Outside it was
"a hell of a life aboard of a destroyer":

Droppin' ash-cans, that's our game. . . .
If we hit our own "subs," it's all the same—
Oh, it's a hell of a life aboard of a destroyer.

An obliging sergeant pointed out a ganglin' yellow boy
(one who had just been relieved) as the chief singer of the

Georgia song. . . . With a little encouragement he sang the solo parts while some other members of his shift harmonized the refrains. . . . It was a "going home" song, one they had surely sung many times. . . . They sang it in a dreamy, unconfident manner—perchance it had been too long coming true.

Six million soldiers—standin' side by side. . . .
Better have a mighty ship 'cause I'm sure goin' to ride. . . .
Back home to Georgia—Georgia . . .
Back to my beau lover gal in Georgia.

(The fact that there were less than two million Americans at the most engaged in the war didn't seem to matter to this rhymster.)

Never goin' to eat no more army food—
Goin' to git myself up like a regular dark-town dude—
Back home in Georgia—Georgia . . .
Back to my beau lover gal in Georgia.

Hope we're never goin' to have another goddam gare—
'Cause if we do, de "drafters" sho' will never find me
    there. . . .
Back home in Georgia—Georgia. . . .
Back to my beau lover gal in Georgia.

(In other words, if war is ever declared again, he'll be so far away, it will take twenty-five cents to send him a postcard.)

White folks says a slacker's done married off my skirt—
If this be so, I sho' Lord will do somebody dirt. . . .
Back home in Georgia—Georgia. . . .
Back to my beau lover gal in Georgia.

GEORGIA

ARRANGED BY J. J. N.

⊕ Chorus

Geor - gia, Geor - gia, back to my beaux lov - er gal in

Geor - gia. Six mil-lion sol - diers stand - in' side by side;

Bet - ter have a might-y ship, 'cause I'm sure goin' to ride back home to

Next morning, as we were about to leave camp for the last time, some one came running from the Headquarters building with a sheaf of orders.

"GEORGIA"

"Any of you men want to go to Poland? Poland—any officer below the rank of major—aviators preferred."

"You mean Poland, Pennsylvania."

"Aw, hell, no. . . . Why go to Poland, Pennsylvania? No, what I'm gettin' at is the original Poland—where they're fightin' . . ."

"Oh, yes, where the war is. . . ."

Every one paused while a silver two-franc piece spun into
the air and landed tails up in the dust. . . . As far as I can
tell, he may be there yet looking for some one to go to
Poland—where the war was. . . . After all, we'd been to
almost all the really interesting places, and none of us was
willing to give up a nice free ride on a ship like the *Cap
Finistère* for the prospects of a two-by-four war in Poland.